Making Information Available
in Digital Format:
Perspectives from Practitioners

Edited by Professor Terry Coppock

Aplications for reproduction should be made to
The Stationery Office Limited
St Crispins
Duke Street
Norwich
NR3 1PD

First published 1999

British Library Cataloguing in Publication Data
A catalogue record for this book is available from the British Library

ISBN 0 11 497276 1

Acknowledgments

Thanks are due to many people for the success of the symposium on which this volume is based - to the five sponsoring organizations for financial support, to the members of the Organizing Committee (Professor Beck, Peter Burnhill, Reg De Mellow, Dr Anne Matheson, Ian McGowan, George MacKenzie and Seamus Ross, three of whom contributed -papers) for their help and wise advice in securing the participation of very busy people, to those people listed on the contents page for producing their contributions to time, despite the heavy pressures upon them and a very tight timetable for publication, to Heather Mantell, Meetings Secretary of the Royal Society of Edinburgh, who made the administrative arrangements and her colleagues at the Society for a very successful and productive symposium, and to Jane McNair of The Stationery Office for her understanding and handling of the tight schedule for publication.

The Organising Committee is grateful for a generous grant towards the cost of publication, kindly provided by ICL UK Limited.

List of speakers

Professor Sir John Arbuthnott, Principal and Vice Chancellor, University of Strathclyde McCance Building, 1 Richmond St, Glasgow, G1
email: j.arbuthnott@mrs.strath.ac.uk

Peter Burnhill, Director, EDINA, and Head, Data Library, University of Edinburgh, Computer Services, University Library, George Square, Edinburgh, EH8
email: edina@ed.ac.uk

Dr Ian Carter, Deputy Director, Research and Development, University of Glasgow, Glasgow, G12 8QQ
email: i.carter@enterprise.gla.ac.uk

Professor Terry Coppock, Secretary and Treasurer, Carnegie Trust for the Universities of Scotland, Cameron House, Abbey Park Place, Dunfermline, Fife KY12 7PZ
email: carnegie.trust@ed.ac.uk

Nancy E Elkington, Research Library Group Member Initiatives, University of London Library, Senate House, Malet St, London, WC1E 7HU
email: nancyelkington@notes.reg.org

George MacKenzie, National Archive of Scotland, HM General Register House, Edinburgh, EH1 3YY
email: gmackenzie@nas.gov.uk

Professor Bob Morris, Department of economic and Social History, University of Edinburgh, William Robertson Building, George Square, Edinburgh, EH8 9JY
email: rjmorris@ed.ac.uk

Dr R G W Prescott, Director, Scottish Institute of Maritime Studies, School of History, University of St Andrews, St Andrews, Fife, KY16 9AJ
email: rgwprescott@st.andrews.ac.uk

Dr Norman Reid, Keeper of Manuscripts, St Andrews University Library, North Street, St Andrews, Fife, KY16 9TR
email: normanreid@st.andrews.ac.uk

Dr Seamus Ross, Director, Humanities, Computing and Information Management, Faculty of Arts, 11 University Gardens, Glasgow, G12 8QQ
email: s.ross@arts.gla.ac.uk

Professor Bruce Royan, Chief Executive, SCRAN (Scottish Cultural Resources Access Network), Abden House, 1 Marchall Crescent, Edinburgh, EH16 5HU
email: rbruce@scran.ac.uk

Dr Nigel Thorp, Director, Centre for Whistler Studies, Glasgow University Library, Hillhead Street, Glasgow, G12 8QE
email: n.thorp@whistler.arts.gla.ac.uk

CONTENTS

Introduction

Terry Coppock
Carnegie Trust for the Universities of Scotland
Dunfermline

As Scotland enters the digital age, there is increasing encouragement in Higher Education to adopt information technology - in teaching, research, administration. The availability of information in machine-readable form is important for both teaching and research. In some fields, such information, often collected by government agencies as part of some administrative procedure, is already available, although it still has to be structured and managed if it is to be useful to those in Higher Education; but there are also vast resources which exist in analogue form and which would increase greatly in flexibility and usefulness if they could be converted into digital form, particularly those concerning aspects of Scotland's cultural heritage   It is not therefore surprising that the Carnegie Trust for the Universities of Scotland should be receiving an increasing number of applications for grants to convert analogue records of various kinds into digital form; some concerned specific sources, such as the Reid Manuscripts at Aberdeen University, while others were national resources of use to a wide variety of scholars, such as the Scottish National Dictionary. It was clear that many applicants had little experience of such projects and the Executive Committee of the Trust reacted positively to a suggestion that a symposium be held to bring together potential applicants and experts on the creation and management of digital resources.

The Trust prefers not to be the sole funder of such projects - its role is often to supply seed corn or to help set the process of fund-raising under way. The proposal to hold such a symposium was put by the Trust to a number of national bodies with an interest in digital records - Edinburgh Data Information Access (EDINA), the National

Library for Scotland, the National Archives of Scotland, the Royal Society of Edinburgh and the Scottish Higher Education Funding Council - each of which offered support and contributed members to an Organizing Committee under my chairmanship. The Symposium, with the title *Creating Scholarly Resources in the Digital Age; Unlocking the Nation's Riches,* was hosted on 18th November by the Royal Society of Edinburgh, whose Meetings Secretary made the administrative arrangements.

It is increasingly clear that not all the vast quantity of material in analogue form can be digitized, not least because of the huge cost of converting it and archiving it. It is equally clear that such projects must have regard for the wide use of the resulting products and that there must be national and local strategies for selecting those that are likely to be most valuable. The digital data must be managed efficiently both to facilitate access and to ensure their survival, their quality must be ensured and their collection and storage fully documented for the benefit of both present and future users. Funding must also be considered, for little progress can be made if such projects are not properly funded.

The programme was directed to addressing these concerns. Five experts, with long experience in this field, distilled that experience for the benefit of prospective applicants. Dr Seamus Ross, as Director of Humanities Computing and Information Management at Glasgow University and formerly Assistant Secretary for Information Technology at the British Academy, tackled the question of selecting resources for digitization; Professor Bruce Royan, Chief Executive of The Scottish Cultural Resources Access Network, used SCRAN's experience in managing nearly three hundred project, to describe the process of managing a typical project; Nancy Elkington, from the Research Libraries Group, created imaginative scenarios of the needs of future researchers in order to focus on the best ways of preserving digital information; Peter Burnhill, Director of EDINA, one of three national centres funded by the Joint Information Systems

Committee, and Head of the Data Library at Edinburgh University, focused on issues of accessing digital resources; and Dr Ian Carter, Deputy Director of Research and Enterprise at Glasgow University, gave advice based on long experience of receiving and processing applications for funding such projects.

The other component of the programme comprised shorter accounts of work in progress on four projects. Dr Nigel Thorp, Director of the Centre for Whistler Studies at Glasgow University, described the creation of a database of some 12,000 letters and their conversion into electronic form; Dr Norman Reid , Keeper of Manuscripts in the Library of St Andrews University, explored the substantial photographic archives held by Aberdeen, Dundee and St Andrews Universities and their conversion into digital form to provide both easier access and the preservation of a fragile resource; Dr Robert Prescott, Director of the National Historic Ships Project at St Andrews University, described the creation of a database of all surviving British-built ships over 40 feet long or with a displacement of over 40 tons, launched before 1945 and substantially intact, to assist management of this historic resource and the selection of vessels for preservation; and George MacKenzie, of the National Archives of Scotland, who outlined the creation of a database of all Scottish wills up to 1875 and of digital images which will be accessible via the Internet and an important source of both historic data and images. Additionally, Professor Bob Morris, of the Department of Social and Economic History in the University of Edinburgh, drew on his extensive experience of studying the social history of Scotland to examine the use of national and local digital records in nominal record linkage.

The symposium, and this volume, concludes with remarks by Professor Sir John Arbuthnott, Principal and Vice-Chancellor of the University of Strathclyde, who was Chairrnan of the Joint Information Systems Committee for four years when policies on digital libraries were emerging. To provide a symmetry to this symposium and to this volume, he will succeed me as Secretary of this Trust in the Millennial Year.

Strategies for Selecting Resources for Digitization:
Source-Orientated, User-Driven, Asset-Aware Model (SOUDAAM)

Seamus Ross
Humanities Advanced Technology
and Information Institute (HATII)
University of Glasgow

Introduction

The conversion of analogue materials into digital form is a labour-intensive and time-consuming process in which attention must be paid not only to the processes of description, storage, distribution and long-term retention, but also to the issues of selection, collection risk, and user needs. Many digitization projects have so far been based on selecting the best items from a collection, on choosing material of interest to a particular archivist, curator, librarian or researcher or on converting material for which funding sources could be easily identified. While in the early days of digitization this approach had much to commend itself, now that the landscape of creation, delivery and use has changed it is important that the selection of material for representation in digital form be subject to systematic and thoughtful planning. Four key parameters could provide a framework to structure efforts to identify and select material that could be digitized. All digitization programmes should be based on:

- an analysis of conventional holdings and strategic planning of digital collection development on institutional, regional and national levels;
- source oriented reviews of collections;
- institutions establishing whether the newly created digital

materials would complement other local, regional or national digital resources or leverage their conversion; and,

- estimating the level of user demand - whether for enjoyment, teaching and learning, or research - as this provides a crucial benchmark in establishing, if only crudely, the potential impact of digitization.

This paper examines these and a matrix of other issues which can assist those designing digitization programmes in justifying their decisions to digitize certain materials first rather than others. It stresses that all programmes of digitization should recognize the value of the asset, the qualities of individual sources, and the needs of users. These are the key elements of a Source-Orientated, User-Driven, Asset-Aware Model (SOUDAAM).

Digital Representation an Interpretative Process

In Tom Stoppard's play *The Invention of Love* a young A.E. Housman meets Benjamin Jowett, the Classicist and at the time of their meeting Master of Balliol College (1997, 24-6). A lively debate ensues between the two about the transcription of words in a poem of Catullus and the difficulties with textual transmission across space and time. Jowett brings to life for the audience the process by which errors had, with each copying, crept into the manuscript tradition. By the time of its first printing more than 1500 years after Catullus' death the poems had been copied many times by scribes of varying skill, judgment, dedication, honesty and attentiveness. There could be little doubt that the manuscripts had become rich with scribal errors. Even the process of rendering the poems in moveable type, which made it possible to deliver near identical copies to a wider audience, produced a further instance where error could be introduced into the text as the printer laid out the type. The causes of error can be, in this instance, attributed to the mode of transcription—human intervention.

When we think about representing analogue information in digital form the process by which information can be lost, so obvious to classical and medieval scholars, becomes less obvious. We forget that **digitization**, the process by which information stored in analogue format is converted into a digitally-encoded form, is not copying, it **is sampling**. It involves the use of technology to capture and represent the information currently stored in analogue formats as a sequence of 0s and 1s. These binary digits, bits, can be stored, manipulated, and presented with computers and other devices (e.g., audio CD-ROM player) capable of handling/interpreting digitally encoded data. This process of sampling applies to digitally representing audio (see, for instance, Digital Sound 1994), moving images, printed matter (whether brittle books or photographs), manuscripts, and a range of other materials. In this process information is lost and artefacts can be inserted. Some parameters influencing the correspondence between the analogue original and the digital representation are obvious. The decision to select a particular sampling rate of, for instance, 600 dpi (dots per inch) and 24-bit colour will render the digital image in more detail than a sampling rate of 300 dpi and 8-bit colour. Of course this is a decision over which the end user has control, but the process of digitization has many 'black box' aspects to it that influence quality and are either beyond our control or frequently overlooked.

In digital imaging, the work environment, lighting, skills of the staff, management of workflow, and guidelines for handling the analogue materials are all general factors that are easily within our control. Other factors over which we have some control, but which can be overlooked, include the quality of the digital cameras and scanners and their components—CCD (Charged Couple Devices) arrays, light sources, digital signal processors and optical elements. Many of these factors are hidden from the user and only detailed analysis of the technical documentation about the equipment and metric testing will make them evident. In the arts, humanities and the cultural sphere the legal risk of our failure to address the shortcomings of the equipment are minimal. In areas such as radiography and structural analysis the precision of the digital images is essential, has evidential value, and could lead, if it could be shown that erroneous decisions were taken based upon images captured with poorly calibrated or technically inferior equipment, to legal actions (see radiology journal, *Digital Imaging*). The technology is undergoing rapid change and the possibilities and ways we can study our existing holdings continue to evolve. Our research expectations are also evolving.

Numerous authors have sought to clarify what aims we might achieve through digitizing our collections (Digitisation of Library...1999; Kenney 1996). Most recently Abbey Smith has, in her essay *Why Digitise*, pressed the argument that digitization is one tool in the workbox of librarians, archivists and museum professionals to better manage and improve use of the collections in their care (1999). Generally the primary justifications for digital representation are enhanced access across space and time and better conservation. Rarely can digitization be seen as a preservation medium; it can be viewed as a conservation aid where it reduces wear-and-tear on the original. In cases where the analogue medium itself is degrading and conservation methods to either stabilise or reverse the process are not available then it is likely that a digital copy might provide a suitable preservation medium (e.g., brittle books, but see Kenney 1998 and others). There are other reasons. Digital images of material can bring functional benefits. They can enhance collaborative working through the sharing of materials between distributed scholars and they can be investigated using a range of image analysis tools that are becoming increasingly sophisticated (Ross 1995, xix-xxi). By beginning with a survey of the collection and a study of complementary collections it may be possible to bring together virtually distributed collections. The Dunhuang Project has this as one of its objectives (Whitfield 1998).

At the very outset those considering embarking on digitisation projects should ask 'why does our institution wish to digitize from its holdings.' If the answer that comes back is because everyone else is doing it, then stop and think again. Unless your institution needs to enhance access to its holdings, improve their research potential, can justify digitization for conservation means, or can demonstrate that digitization will enhance research or teaching and learning either by providing materials for primary, secondary or the higher education communities it should not proceed.

Digital Collection Development Plans

It is evident that researchers, institutions caring for collections, and funding agencies need a schematic model for handling the decision making activities associated with selection and prioritization of holdings for digital representation. There have been numbers of attempts to create models of this kind (Chapman *et al.*. 1997; Columbia University Libraries 1997; Hazen, *et al.*. 1998; Kenney 1998; NLDP Project Planning Checklist 1997; Parry 1998; Towards a Learning Nation... 1997). These work with varying degrees of adequacy. After studying these models a reviewer is left wondering what should be the key components of a selection model. A model should:

- focus on collection conservation requirements and audience needs;
- incorporate activities to establish the needs of the user communities and ensure that these needs are reflected in the decision making process;
- be applicable across all analogue media types (i.e., paper, manuscripts, audio, moving images, and three-dimensional objects);
- respond to institutional research objectives and public access driven needs;
- provide a framework for institutions to define the intellectual, historic, cultural and physical value of their assets;
- focus attention of institutions on undertaking a detailed

study of their collections and encourage them to build on that survey;
- respond to technological possibilities and obsolescence;
- recognize that researchers and institutions will carry out most of their digitization activities as discrete projects and provide strategies for amalgamating these into programmes; and,
- respond to issues of intellectual property rights (IPR).

Selection and prioritization tend to be, in many institutions, informal processes even when the institution applies selection guidelines. Surprisingly few institutions preparing to embark on digitization have prepared a statement describing the character and extent of their own collections and how these collections interrelate both within their institution and to holdings at other institutions. This is in part because many institutions lack a strategic plan for creating digital representations of their holdings. This plan, known as a Digital Collection Development Plan (DCDP) consists of two elements, an Intellectual Asset Survey (IAS) and a Digital Representation Implementation Plan (DRIP). Many institutions need to become familiar with their collections through detailed study of them before embarking on any attempts to digitize their holdings. Most of this work should begin with a strategic survey of the institution's collections—a detailed analysis of the holdings and their intellectual, cultural, social, curatorial and public values. The process of building an Intellectual Asset Survey (IAS) should involve keepers of analogue holdings, academic researchers, educationalists, legal professionals, and general users. The complexity of such a survey will vary from institution to institution. For academic institutions with their diverse activities, the variety of their holdings and the numbers of content creators working in them, such a survey will be a complex process. This complexity will increase with the size and research breadth of the academic institution concerned. In academic institutions potentially valuable assets will reside outside such traditional content curating centres as the library, archives and museum. Departments, research institutes, and laboratories often house valuable data that are overlooked and lost by institutions lacking a robust intellectual asset strategy.

Following the survey of the information assets, the planning turns to the development of an implementation programme. This involves examining such factors as the skills-base, current state of technology, and user needs for research, teaching and public enjoyment. In this process the institution should investigate whether it has sufficient technical infrastructure and the capabilities to develop and enforce policies and legal instruments that protect the digital versions of their assets.

Ensuring that there is correspondence between the institutional strategic plan and the Digital Collection Development Plan (DCDP) is essential, if the DCDP is to be implemented successfully. Defining how the plan will fit into other regional and national strategic plans and initiatives will further increase the likelihood that the DCDP will be successfully implemented. The DCDP and its components, the IAS and the Digital Representation Implementation Plan (DRIP), should be ratified and adopted as institutional policy.

In considering collections for digitization, holders might conclude that some of their holdings were not acceptable for representation in digital form for a number of reasons. Institutions often hold material that is inappropriate for digitization because it is, for instance, defamatory, obscene, or culturally insensitive or offensive. While there may be good archival and collection reasons for retaining this material for posterity the justifications for representing it in digital form may be far less evident. The analogue form of these materials facilitates the ability of institutions to control access to their content through controlling access to the objects themselves; once digitally represented this becomes difficult. Some holdings are not suitable for conversion because they have low intellectual content and their digitization would bring little research,

11

teaching, or public benefit. Other holdings are in such poor physical condition that the processes of digitization, such as handling and light exposure, may put them at excessive risk. For these materials there is a delicate balancing act to be achieved between the conservation benefits of providing access to digital facsimiles and the risk to which the originals may be put in the course of data capture. On the other hand the risks posed by technology decrease annually, and will continue to lessen for the foreseeable future, although it will be some time before it can be said that digitization poses no risks to the assets being captured.

A part of digital collection development planning involves establishing what are the user communities that will take advantage of these digital assets. Examining usage of current analogue collections often forms the basis of selecting material for conversion. Material in low demand in the analogue collection is in this way less likely to be digitized. The argument that material in low demand should be given limited priority in digitisation strategies is, however, specious. Often collections are not used because they are little known. Once they are available in digital form their use increases dramatically. For some collections of material that are easier to use when represented in digital form the process of digitization is transformative. Digitization places holdings in an environment that can ease their discovery, retrieval, manipulation, presentation and analysis.

Institutional collections will include much material in which the institution does not hold the intellectual property rights (IPR). Where the institution does not own these rights and where it has no way of easily securing a perpetual license to exploit the asset in digital form other assets should be selected for digitization. As the collections are among the intellectual assets of an institution every effort must be made to secure the institution's rights as their owner. A first step in this process is for institutions to develop model license agreements to maintain institutional control of the digital assets.

This is the point at which policies for access should be defined. These might consider such questions as:

- will external users be given access to low-resolution images for research and teaching purposes?
- will internal users be permitted to use the high-resolution digital assets for research and teaching?
- what policies and charges will govern external use of high-resolution images, or high fidelity audio?
- what policies will be implemented covering use by members of staff of digital material in electronic publications produced by other institutions or commerical publishers?

Although technology may eventually ease the process of identifying instances where the rights of institutions in digital images or audio have been infringed, it can be very difficult unless your institution is a large corporation to identify and pursue those who have infringed your rights in digital materials. License agreements, the use of digital watermarks (generated at the point and time of access and embedded dynamically and uniquely in each audio or image file), and encryption are three tools that can assist in securing intellectual capital (Berghel and O'Gorman 1996; Johnson and Jajodia 1998).

The initial development stages are the right time to address the problems associated with archiving digital materials. Until fairly recently computing service staff equated archiving with backing-up. It is widely agreed, at long last, that these two terms are very different. To back-up is to make a copy of digital material on to other, and usually portable, media that can be secured (often off-site) to provide a recovery path in the event that the system from which the back-up was taken lost data through either hardware or software failure, human error, virus attack, or disaster. Back-ups are intended for near term security. Archiving reflects a long-term strategy to ensure the availability of digital assets for decades, if not centuries

13

(RLG/CPA 1996; Ross 1997; Ross 1998; Ross and Gow 1999; Rothenberg 1995).

While arts and humanities research remains driven by problem orientation, the process of research is changing (Ross 1999). It is becoming more collaborative, dependent upon the use of technological tools and it depends more and more on technical support. Moreover there is an increasing emphasis on the verifiability of research through the testing, and re-testing, of hypotheses and conclusions against the data used by the original researcher. This adds weight to the need to address the problems associated with ensuring the authenticity and reliability of digital data. It is widely recognized that information once created in digital form should be re-used wherever possible across a range of projects (Ross 1995; BL/BA 1993).

It is worth considering that many of the issues raised by these digitization or content creation projects have arisen in the face of other technologies and media. An illustrious comparison might be drawn with the late eighth and early ninth century cultural and intellectual revolution known as the Carolingian Renaissance. This renaissance was predicated on training, standardization, com-munication, and access to authenticated sources. Standardization, for instance, played an important role as the scriptoria across Charlemagne's Empire, beginning in the 780s, adopted a new script, Carolingian minuscule, consisting of separated and regularly well-formed letters (Bischoff 1965, Bischoff 1990). The accuracy and authenticity of their sources was of immense concern to late eighth- and ninth-century thinkers and new copies of manuscripts which were created in accordance to the 'guidelines', and I use the term loosely, were marked ex authentico libro. The concentration of the Carolingians on the creation of accurate and verified transmission arose from the realization that the quality and verisimilitude of their sources was central to the quality of their understanding.

Debates still rage about the preservation role of digitization. In analogue sources much information exists which cannot be captured by the current generation of digitization equipment. This applies to all classes of material: still and moving images, audio, and three-dimensional objects. Source-orientation ensures that the conservation needs of the collection are observed and that the technologies used for digitization are appropriate to the sources.

Financial and technological constraints may limit the ability of an institution or researcher to proceed with the implementation of a digitization strategy developed following the collection survey. On the other hand, having a strategic plan in place will ensure that institutions can respond coherently when new technological opportunities arise. The process of representing analogue sources in digital form involves the availability of suitable capture technologies (e.g., digital cameras, scanners), digital signal processing, storage facilities, manipulation, access, delivery, use, standards, security, and charging policies and technologies. A detailed discussion of these issues is outside the scope of this paper, but see http://www.hatii. arts.gla.ac.uk/Courses/CultHerComp/URLsFrames.htm for pointers. The DRIP is the place to establish guidelines for the digitization of materials in the collections—for instance it would cover such factors as bit-depth and resolution for imaging and sampling rates for audio to mention just two. Technology is a fast moving target. Often projects opt for scanning at colour and resolution levels that match today's delivery technology. This is a mistaken approach as these projects are not future proof even for the medium term.

This is also the stage at which to consider whether the documentation systems, catalogues, or finding aids are of suitable calibre to provide a backbone for the digital assets. Institutions need to establish in their DRIP guidelines for description of digital objects, a definition of the metadata categories required (e.g., discovery, management, and preservation metadata), rules for metadata creation, and policies governing access.

The physical qualities of the source material are of critical importance. The dimensions, type and nature, condition, structure (e.g., mounted, bound), light sensitivities, production process, tonal range, and presence or absence of colour are only a small number of parameters that need to be considered when planning to digitize analogue materials such as printed and manuscripts. A range of comparable factors deserves consideration when plans and process descriptions are drawn up for the digitization of audio, moving images, and three-dimensional objects.

There is a whole range of approaches to structuring a digitization project. Projects might digitize along media and material types, or seek to cut across collections and focus on bringing together interdependent and interrelated materials. The former approach is common for projects that either focus on categories of material, such as photographic holdings or specialized types of media, such as ethnographic recordings. The latter approach is typified by projects that focus on particular themes, subject areas, or historic periods. On occasion research, teaching and public benefit may not be the foremost justification for prioritizing holdings for digitization and it may be institutional marketing or development priorities that come to the fore. A decision might be taken to represent a specific analogue gift in digital form, in the hope that this might leverage other donors to deposit their holdings at the institution.

For institutions with small collections the process of prioritizing the material selected for digital representation is unlikely to prove a difficult task. Larger institutions may find that even once the material has been selected it will need to be placed in an order of priority to maximize investment and scarce labour and financial resources. The collection strategy will form the basis of a prioritization of resources for the digitization programme. The process of prioritization itself can be approached from a number of vantage points. The following questions may help with prioritization:

- Would making the material available diminish or enhance the value of the underlying collection?
- Would conversion of the material leverage the opening up of material in other collections?
- Have other projects digitized complementary material?
- Is the material unique?
- Is there an existing demand for the material?
- Will digitization create a demand for the material?
- Will the digital content be capable of being reused for multiple purposes?
- Will it be necessary or possible to monitor how the material is used?
- Would digital representation assist in the conservation of the material?
- Is there potential for commercial exploitation where such exploitation would not diminish the value of the item or collection?
- Does the material have untapped research potential?
- Would the improved functionality that digitization would bring enhance the research potential of the item or collection?
- Could the material play a role as a teaching resource?
- Would digitization lead to financial savings through reducing infrastructure and labour costs associated with supporting collection management and access?
- Would digitization have publicity benefits?
- Is the current generation of technology suitable or would it be better to wait?

Since the end of the Second World War there has been an increasing emphasis on audio and visual resources. This transition has been expedited to a remarkable extent by the increasing ease of using computers and the development of the Internet. This has increased the level of interest in photographic collections. Many institutions have acquired substantial collections. Current initiatives are converting these into digital form. Individually they are little more than picture collections, but if this process were part of a larger attempt to digitize holdings to create a visual digital record of the late nineteenth and twentieth centuries from a number of thematic vantage points the whole process would be radically different.

One obvious drawback of the strategic approach to retroconverting collections is that much scholarship is done by individual scholars who are seeking answers to intellectually challenging problems in their specialism. Increasingly institutions are defining umbrella institutional research strategies and expecting departments to have research strategies at local level which reflect these institutionally-led objectives. Similarly, given the high cost of creating digital assets of enduring value, research strategies need to take into account the institutional collections and inform, and be informed by, strategies to represent them in digital form. This is particularly the case in the United Kingdom where there are currently (1999) a number of initiatives offering funding for the digitization of material for educational and research purposes. In many sectors the availability of funding for the generation of digital materials has become a driving force, which has led many professionals to dash lemming-like into digitisation. As a result many projects are poorly planned and will create assets of either short-term usefulness or no value at all. Projects therefore must focus on creating sustainable resources that will be reusable in the face of changing technology and be part of scalable programmes. Funding agencies recognize this now and put emphasis on sustainability of assets and the application of best practices and standards. These agencies will increasingly find that 'a national strategy is needed for the conversion of analogue material into digital form' an idea expressed over six years ago now in the report on *Information Technology in Humanities Scholarship* prepared on behalf of the British Library and the British Academy (BL/BA 1993, 33).

Unlocking the Full Potential of Collections

Digitization through imaging, digitizing of sound and moving images does not fully unlock the full potential of the sources (BL/BA 1993; Townsend, *et al.* 1999). Digitization addresses only a small part of the creation of digital resources for research and teaching purposes. Much of the material that is imaged is not suitable for Optical Character Recognition (OCR): some is hand-written, some is in typefaces that current OCR software cannot handle (e.g., blackletter), some is skewed, and some has been imaged at too low a quality to provide the necessary data for the OCR engines to convert the textual digital images into text. In other instances digital representation does not present the resource in ways that make it feasible to use them to maximum potential. Street directories, voting registers, and memberships lists so valuable to historians, like many other documents, achieve their full research potential only when they are encoded in data structures that support their manipulation as discrete information units rather than image elements.

Currently content-based image retrieval is not sufficiently robust to provide the tools scholars require to investigate the digital images themselves. This is true of both moving and still images (Gudivada and Raghavan 1995). There is strong evidence from case studies, such as the work conducted by NASA to investigate digital images of the earth taken by satellites using their Image Understanding Environment tools or that done by Das, Manmatha, and Riseman on indexing flower patents (1999), that in the longer term this problem will be cracked. Numerous other case studies could be cited, but two further examples will suffice, the work of the IBM team which has developed Query by Image and Video Content (QBIC) (Flickner, *et al.* 1995) and video retrieval studies (Chang *et al.* 1997, Yeo and Yeung 1998). What is evident is that during the coming decade researchers will bring on stream tools that will revolutionize how we study digital resources, but for the foreseeable future scholarly use of resources will remain dependent on their analysis, abstraction and encoding (Eakins and Graham 1999).

The question that we must ask ourselves is whether or not the digital images that we are creating will have been created to a high-enough standard that they could be used in the digital research laboratory. If they are not then the original analogue materials will need to be captured digitally again. Whether those planning projects decide that it is more expedient to select standards against current technology or to attempt to produce the highest quality images today so that they could form the basis of resources for the future will reflect a trade-off between near and long term costs.

Establishing strategies and guidelines for quality assurance is an essential step in creating a DRIP. In the case of images, Reilly and Frey (1996) point out:

There are no guidelines or accepted standards for determining the level of image quality required in the creation of databases for access or preservation of photographic, microphotographic, or document collections. As a result, many institutions now starting their scanning projects will be disappointed sooner or later, because their choices did not take into account future changes in the technology (1996, 18).

They go on to explain that:

Image quality is usually separated into two classes:
- *Objective* image quality is evaluated through physical measurements of image properties. In the case of digital imaging this is achieved with special software evaluating the digital file.
- *Subjective* image quality is evaluated through judgement by human observers (*ibid.,* 19).

While psychometric measures provide one approach other more objective metrics include tone, colour, detail and edge reproduction and noise. All researchers agree that we are still at an early point in establishing metrics for evaluating the quality of digital images. Those metrics which might be suitable for quality assuring images for visual study by humans may not prove sufficient for digital images that are to be analysed using software tools. The key question is what will be the minimum sample that different computer-based analysis tools will require if digital images are to be rigorously used as an element in the scholarly process (Ross 1999).

It is unlikely that all the materials in our heritage collections will be represented in digital form during the next fifty years. Although in the UK, in a number of countries in continental Europe and in the US, the resources available for digitization and the limited availability of funding will restrict how much material we can convert into digital form.

There are huge gaps in our knowledge about digitization. There is a need for more robust costing models that can handle the entire lifecycle. These models in turn depend upon the existence of workflow models; current models tend to be unrealistic and do not document adequately the activities involved in a digitization project. Digitization and retroconversion are a chain of activities of which selection is one small part (Tanner and Robinson 1998; Kenney 1998). It is nevertheless an essential part. While these activities produce new assets they consume scarce resources. To ensure that the quality and viability of these resources is adequate more research is needed in the areas of lighting, technology selection, long-term preservation of digital assets, and the evaluation of user needs and usage of digital collections. There is a need for a digital asset register, which documents not only completed projects, but also ongoing ones. This will form an essential plank in efforts to avoid unnecessary duplication of effort.

Conclusions

Funding agencies need to consider funding work only at institutions that have a Digital Collection Development Plan (DCDP) in place and can demonstrate how these activities will fit into the other regional and national objectives.

Institutions and even individual researchers are encouraged to adopt a source-orientated user-driven asset-aware model (SOUDAAM) for the identification, selection, and prioritization of material for digitization and retroconversion.

- At a strategic level institutions need to define the objectives that they wish to achieve through the digitization of their holdings. Are these enhanced research performance, increased publicity for the institution of its holdings, the creation of income generating assets, improved conservation of holdings through the provision of surrogates, reduction of staff levels by shifting the provision of access to holdings from the original objects to virtual representations, or a combination of all these objectives.
- Institutions should draw up Digital Collection Development Plans before embarking on any future projects of digital representation.
- The needs of users, whether these are students, researchers or the general public, must be considered.
- The condition and conservation needs of collections must be audited and a risk assessment produced.

With these four categories of information it will be feasible to lay the ground for a programme to represent institutional holdings in digital form. Technology poses the next obstacle; it needs to be appropriate. Some objectives outlined in the DCDP will prove impossible given available technology. The strategic plan must respond to the technology and its implementation must depend upon an iterative decision making process which considers user and technology implications at each stage. If institutions acknowledge that the intellectual capital that they hold is an asset of similar calibre to their estates and buildings the need for strategic planning and controlled implementation of those plans becomes self-evident. The focus should be on the production of high-quality resources that will transform access and the functionality of research collections.

Activities of this kind enable institutions to exploit the research and income potential of their intellectual capital. Institutions should bear in mind that the competition for the attention of potential users is becoming more intense as the quantities of data expand. This will have an impact on projected income streams. Those collections that have been strategically selected, digitally represented at the highest quality and have robust documentation and discovery tools associated with them stand the best chance of remaining prominent in this new environment.

References

These are to both books and articles and to web sites; the latter are highlighted by an asterisk

Berghel, H. and O'Gorman, L. (1996), Protecting ownership rights through digital watermarking, *Computer* July 29 (7): 101-103.

Bischoff, B. (1965) Die Karolingische Minuskel, In Braunfels, W. (ed), *Karl der Grosse: Werk und Wirkung*, Aachen, 1965.

—(1990) *Latin Palaeography: Antiquity and the Middle Ages.* Cambridge.

[BL/BA] (1993) *Information Technology in Humanities Scholarship: British Achievements, Prospects, and Barriers,* The British Library Research and Development Department and The British Academy, London.

Chang, S-F., Chen, W., H.J., Sundaram, H., and Zhong, D. (1997), VideoQ an automated content based video search system using visual cues. *Proceedings of the ACM Conference on Multimedia '97,* 313-324.

Chapman, S. et al., 1997. Selection for Digitizing: A Decision Making Matrix, May 1997
http://preserve.harvard.edu/resources/digitization/matrix.html

*Columbia University Libraries, (1997). Selection criteria for digital imaging projects
http://www.columbia.edu/cu/libraries/digital/criteria

Das, M., Manmatha, R., and Riseman, E.M. (1999) Indexing flower patent images using domain knowledge, *IEEE Intelligent Systems,* (September/October), 14(5), 24-33.

*Digital Sound,
http://ei.cs.vt.edu/~netinfo/notes/chap1/digitalsound/digsnd.html

*Digitisation of Library Materials: Report of the Concentration Meeting & Workshop Luxembourg, 14.12.98 (1998)
http://www.echo.lu/digicult/en/digit.pdf

*Eakins, J.P. and Graham, M.E. 1999. *Content-based Image Retrieval: A report to the JISC Technology Applications Programme,* Institute for Image Data Research, University of Northumbria at Newcastle.
http://www.unn.ac.uk/iidr/research/cbir/report.html

Flickner, M. et al. (1995), Query by Image and Video Content: The QBIC System, *Computer* 28 (9), 23-32.

Gudivada, V. N. and Raghavan, V. V. (1995), Content-Based Image Retrieval Systems, *Computer* 28 (9), 18-22.

Hazen, D., Horrell, J., and Merrill-Oldham, J. (1998). *Selecting Research Collections for Digitisation,* Washington, D.C.

Johnson, N. F. and Jajodia, S. (1998), Exploring steganography: seeing the unseen', *Computer* February 31 (2): 26-34.

Kenney, A.R. (1996), Conversion of traditional source materials into digital form, in Bearman, D. (ed.) *Research Agenda for Networked Cultural Heritage* (Santa Monica: Getty Art History Information Program), 41-7.

*—(1998), Digital to microfilm conversion: A demonstration project 1994-1996 (Final Report to the National Endowment for the Humanities PS-20781-94). [http://www.library.cornell.edu/preservation/com/comfin.html].

Niblack, W. and Flickner, M. (1993), Find me the pictures that look like this: IBM's Image Query Project, *Advanced Imaging*, (April), 32-5.

*NDLP Project Planning Checklist, Library of Congress, National Digital Library Program, *Last updated January 1997* http://memory.loc.gov/ammem/prjplan.html

*Parry, D. (1998), *Virtually New - Creating the Digital Collection: a review of digitisation projects in local authority libraries and archives.* Final Report to the Library and Information Commission. Prepared by Consultants to the Review, Information North, Library and Information Commission, London. [http://www.ukoln.ac.uk/services/lic/digitisation/].

Prescott, A. (1997), The electronic Beowulf and digital restoration, *Literary and Linguistic Computing*, 12 (3): 185-95.

Reilly, J.M., and Frey, F.S. (1996), *Recommendations for the Evaluation of Digital Images Produced from Photographic, Microphotographic, and Various Paper Formats,* Report to the Library of Congress, National Digital Library Project, Contract # 96CLCSP7582.

[RLG/CPA] (1996), *Preserving Digital Information: Report of the Task Force on Archiving of Digital Information*, (Washington D.C.: Research Libraries Group and Commission on Preservation and Access).

Ross, S. (1993), From conventional photographs to Digital Resources, *Archaeological Computing Newsletter*, 35: 14-21.

—-(1995), Introduction: networking and humanities scholarship, in Kenna, S. and Ross, S. (eds), *Networking in the Humanities* , xi-xxiv, London.

—- (1997), Consensus, communication, and collaboration: fostering multidisciplinary cooperation in electronic records, in *INSAR (Supplement II), Proceedings of the DLM-Forum on electronic records,* 330-36.

—- (1998), 'The Expanding World of Electronic Information and the Past's Future', in Higgs, E, (ed.), *Historians and Electronic Artefacts,* 6-28, London.

*—-(1999), Changing trains at Wigan: Digital preservation and the future of scholarship, The JISC/NPO Digital Preservation Workshop, 3/4 March 1999, Scarman House, University of Warwick, **http://www.leeds.ac.uk/cedars/OTHER/SRoss.htm**

—- and Gow, A. (1999) *Digital Archaeology: Rescuing Neglected and Damaged Data Resources,*London.

Rothenberg, J. (1995), Ensuring the longevity of digital documents', *Scientific American,* 272(1) (January 1995), 24-9.

*Sharpe, L. H., Ott, M. D. and Fleischhauer, C. (1998) Library of Congress Manuscript Digitisation Demonstration Project, Final Report. **http://memory.loc.gov/ammen/pictel/pictel.pdf**

Smith, A., (1999), *Why Digitize,* (Washington DC: CLIR Report 80).

Stoppard, T. (1997). *The Invention of Love,* New York.

*Tanner, S., and Robinson, B. (1998). JISC Image Digitisation Initiative (JIDI): Feasibility Study (Final Report) **http://heds.herts.ac.uk/Guidance/JIDI_fs.pdf**

*Towards a Learning Nation: the Digital Contribution Recommendations Proposed by the Federal Task Force On Digitization, Final Report, 1997
http://www.nlc-bnc.ca/coopprog/finalreport/eindex.htm

*Townsend, S., Chappell, C. and Struijvé, O. (1999). *Digitising History: A Guide to Creating Digital Resources from Historical Documents. AHDS Guides to Good Practice*
http://hds.essex.ac.uk/g2gp/digitising_history/index.html

Whitfield, S. (1998). A database for cataloguing Chinese and Central Asian manuscripts: The International Dunhuang Project, in Carpenter, L., Shaw, S. and Prescott, A. (eds.) *Towards the Digital Library: The British Library's 'Initiatives for Access' Programme,* The British Library, 166-177. London.

Yeo, B. L. and Yeung, M.M., (1998). Classification, simplification, and dynamic visualization of scene transition graphs for video browsing, in Sethi, I. K. and Jain, R, C. (eds.) *Storage and Retrieval for Image and Video Databases VI*, Proc SPIE 3312, 60-70.

Project Management and Quality Assurance

Bruce Royan
Scottish Cultural Resources Access Network
Edinburgh

Any organization embarking on the creation of digital scholarly resources, needs to ensure that this activity is completed on target and within budget, and that its deliverables are fit for the purpose for which they were intended. The Scottish Cultural Resources Access Network (SCRAN) is a five-year, £15 million initiative to build a networked digital resource base for the study and celebration of Human History and Material Culture in Scotland. Based on the experience of managing nearly 300 SCRAN-funded digitization projects, this paper attempts to describe the process of managing a typical project, from Project Initiation, through Interim Review to final Project Closure. It is the proper business of project management to ensure that no project deliverable is signed off unless it is of a quality appropriate for its intended use, now and into the future, and this paper therefore also describes issues of quality assurance, including the enforcement of standards, and normative and summative evaluation.

The SCRAN Project Guidelines

The web site at http://www.scran.ac.uk (Turner and Buchanan, 1997) is an expression of the first three years of a complex and ambitious project to unlock some of the rich scholarly resources of the Scottish nation, and the hundreds of thousands of text records and tens of thousands of digital objects to which it it already gives access are the first fruits of nearly 300 smaller projects which are contributing to SCRAN, involving museums, libraries, archives and other 'memory organizations', large and small. To ensure that each of these projects runs in a controlled fashion, and that all of the projects are coordinated into a meaningful and effective programme, it has been important to develop and to enforce a consistent set of procedures. Several of the SCRAN staff have been involved in project work for many years, and in our experience, a formal project management methodology is a little like hygiene: its presence is not noticeable when things are going well, but its absence can lead to disaster. It is, however, important that such a methodology should not be overly elaborate or labour-intensive: we subscribe to a saying attributed to Albert Einstein: *'Everything should be expressed in as simple a manner as possible – but no simpler'*.

The senior members of the SCRAN team come from a range of public sector backgrounds where they have worked with a very comprehensive methodology known as Projects IN Controlled Environments (PRINCE) (Bradley, 1993). While PRINCE is excellent for the environments in which it was developed, SCRAN feels that a 'lighter touch' is required for the numerous small projects, involving very small teams, with which SCRAN is typically working, and so it has evolved a set of Project Guidelines, which builds on PRINCE thinking and good practice, but which keeps the bureaucratic aspects to a minimum, and which has been laughingly dubbed as *'The Project Methodology formerly known as PRINCE'*.

The SCRAN Project Guidelines (Turnbull & Buchanan, 1997) are given to each new project team at Project Initiation, and while each project is encouraged to exploit its institution's own project management tools and procedures when these exist, it is a condition of SCRAN Grant-aid that the SCRAN Guidelines should also be adhered to. Thus every SCRAN project works within a similar set of frameworks, definitions and procedures as described below.

Project Environment

Every project is a novel set of activities, in some way unique for the institution(s) which is (are) to carry it out. It is important to consider some of the roles that will need to be played within each institution to ensure that the project can proceed in a timely and controlled fashion.

Project Manager

A senior SCRAN officer is allocated to every SCRAN project, to oversee its work and to provide the main point of contact between the project and SCRAN. The Project Manager is usually assisted in this role by a designated SCRAN Project Officer.

Project Leader

The Contributor Institution(s) nominate(s) an officer who will be responsible for communication with SCRAN and who will complete and sign SCRAN Project Reports.

Project Team

Although Project Leaders may in some circumstances work alone, they are more commonly responsible for coordinating the activities of a number of other people working for or on behalf of Contributor institutions. In projects developing interactive educational products (in SCRAN parlance: Multimedia Essays) as well as discrete digital assets, the team must include one or more educationalist representing the target audience of the projected publication.

Project Board

The PRINCE methodology includes the setting up of a Project Board: a triumvirate of individuals at a sufficiently high level within their institution to be able to make decisions on its behalf and, more importantly, to make commitments of resources and budget to the project. The three roles envisaged under PRINCE are: Senior User (representing the end users of the deliverables from the project - in SCRAN terms perhaps the institution's Education Officer); Senior Technical (representing the areas which have responsibility for implementation – in SCRAN terms perhaps the institution's Head of Documentation); and Executive (providing overall guidance and assessment within the institution's strategic plan - in SCRAN terms, perhaps the Museum Director). SCRAN does not demand that such a board be set up, but it does expect the institutional ownership of the project that such a board would imply. The most frequent reason for projects running into difficulties is insufficient commitment at the institutional level: In the words of Machiavelli (1514)*'It should be borne in mind that there is nothing more difficult to carry out, more doubtful of success, than to initiate a new order of things. The innovator makes enemies of all who profit by the old order, and only lukewarm support is forthcoming from those who would profit from the new . . . people cannot believe in anything new until they have actually experienced it'*

The Project Plan

Once an application for a SCRAN grant has been approved by the Grants Review Committee, the contributor is required to furnish a detailed Project Plan. This plan should contain, as a minimum: a summary of the project indicating its objectives, constraints and target audience; an official start date; names and job descriptions of the key project officers and the tasks they are expected to undertake; arrangements for partnerships or consortia if any; a set of milestones and deliverables (see below); arrangements for quality assurance including trials, pilots and formative or summative evaluations; and a clear reporting procedure. Although this document is very important as the baseline against which project control will be carried out, it is even more useful for necessitating detailed thought about aspects of the project that had not previously been articulated – as Eisenhower is quoted as saying: *'Plans are nothing. Planning is everything'*

Project Initiation

There may in practice be a considerable amount of discussion between the SCRAN team and the contributor before the Project Initiation stage is reached. This is the point marking formal agreement on the scope of the project. A Project Folder is opened (for the filing of all correspondence, file notes, corrective action notes and project reports), an agreed Project Plan is filed into it, a Grant Payment Schedule is created, and a binding Contract issued and signed. At this point an initial Stage Payment (often 30 per cent of the contract value) may be made.

Monitoring and Reporting

Project control methodologies succeed or fail according to the quality of their monitoring and reporting procedures. It has been said that: *'if it were not for the Last Minute, nothing would ever get done'*, and there is certainly nothing like a deadline for concentrating the minds of project workers so as to tie up loose ends and get documentation into place. For SCRAN purposes, Monitoring and Reporting are based on a framework of Milestones, Deliverables and Highlight Reports.

A Milestone is an agreed deadline for the receipt of a defined set of deliverables. A Deliverable is an agreed and identifiable project product. For example, the deliverables at a given milestone might comprise documentation of a selection procedure for material to be digitized, a draft list of the items selected, and a sample set of digitized records for quality testing. Projects are required to hold a meeting at every milestone; the Project Manager reserves the right to attend any such meeting.

Project Highlight Reports must be produced on a monthly basis: in some circumstances, the Project Manager may insist on more frequent reports. The report itself is not intended to be onerous to complete or read: it should be less than one A4 page, in 'bullet point' style, and concentrate on:

Highlights: a summary of the major events (achievements and failures) of the reporting period, concentrating on products delivered, however slight. The section should relate to any items listed for completion, in the Outlook section of previous report.

Outlook: a forecast of progress over the next period, concentrating on any deliverables to be completed, however slight.

Problems: a brief description of any actual or potential problems. Possible remedial actions may also be proposed in this section.

The SCRAN Project Management and Grant Administration team has to keep track of many hundreds of milestones, deliverables and reports for the SCRAN projects, and for this purpose a computer system has been developed which not only records all necessary historical project documentation, but also predicts future events based on the individual project plans. It has been proved to be more effective to remind projects just before a deliverable or report falls due, rather than to chase them up after it has failed to be received.

Quality Assurance

There is little point receiving project deliverables if they are not of appropriate quality. Quality in project deliverables has been described as a little like underlay in fitted carpets: it significantly increases usability and life, but there is no point trying to add it as an afterthought. Quality Assurance may be subdivided into Standards Compliance, Fitness for Purpose, and Business Assurance.

Business Assurance

Business Assurance is a matter of ensuring that appropriate project monitoring and documentation procedures are in place and are being adhered to, signalling any deviations from the project plan and providing reassurance that the overall programme of projects remains compliant with SCRAN's baseline documentation and Business Plan. This function is carried out by an external Project Monitor, appointed by the Millennium Commission, who visits SCRAN quarterly for this purpose.

Documentation Content

Standards Compliance concerns in particular Documentation Content and Digitized Data Quality. Documentation of cultural resources varies in level, structure and vocabulary, depending on the curatorial tradition of the institution that holds it: whether it is in a Library Catalogue, an Archival Finding Aid or a Museum Collection Management System. Though there may be good organizational reasons for this, and though researchers in the material world have long been able to cope with such differences, they would be far from ideal for wider access in the digital arena. The SCRAN Basic Record Standard (Web Site Morrison, 1997) is therefore built upon the Dublin Core Set of Metadata Elements (Web Site OCLC, 1999). Metadata means 'information about information' and the SCRAN record merely provides a pointer, both to the newly digitized object, and to the original documentation, which remains in the holding institution. But insisting on this standard format, irrespective of the domain the object is held in, is one way of increasing access to the resulting resources. To help projects comply with the SCRAN standard, each is supplied with a database system tailored to the computer platform they use, and featuring a SCRAN data entry template.

Data Quality

The quality of the data resulting from any digitization process is a function of the equipment used and the skill of the operator, as well as the size, compression type and data format in which it is stored. The first two aspects are out of the immediate control of SCRAN, but all incoming data are subjected to stringent quality checks, and final grant payment on any project depends on any re-work being satisfactorily completed. Regarding data format issues, however, SCRAN is (in the light of experience) very prescriptive. The SCRAN approach is to demand a format that is a de facto standard and therefore likely to be capable of migration to any future standard. Such a standard may have emerged from a proprietary background, so long as it is not 'tied in' to one supplier: examples being Apple's QuickTime Virtual Reality Format (QTVR) and Adobe's Portable Document Format (PDF). SCRAN also demands the largest possible size of object that can economically be digitized with today's technology. This object will typically be too large for transmission on today's networks or use on today's desktop computers, but is stored off-line as a future-proof archival master and the source of a surrogate tailored for today's network use.

To take images as an example, SCRAN insists that these be scanned within a standard 2048x3072 pixel format, which yields a file size per colour image of 18 Megabytes. This may be delivered as an uncompressed TIFF file, or on a Kodak Photo Compact Disc (PCD). SCRAN staff members check each image, crop it if necessary, adjust for colour balance, brightness, sharpness etc, and then create two surrogates, optimized for network use: a 'thumbnail' image for general web access free of charge, and a screen size image for downloading by educational users in licensed institutions such as universities, schools and public libraries.

Fitness for Purpose

SCRAN is fortunate in being able to call on a range of experts, willing to serve on advisory groups on each of a number of ways in which the emerging SCRAN resource base and delivery service may be judged fit for purpose. Each group contributes to guidelines, provides referees for grant applications, advises on new developments, helps steer evaluation exercises, and provides continuous feedback on SCRAN quality issues.

The Education Advisory group is chaired by the Chief Executive of the Scottish Consultative Committee on the Curriculum and includes teachers, principals, HMIs, educational researchers, and experts on lifelong learning and museum education. Its special interest is the fitness of SCRAN for learning support, and in particular in relation to the Scottish Curriculum Guidelines and the National Grid for Learning.

The Industrial Advisory Group is chaired by the President of the British Computer Society and includes top management from the media, telecommunications, software, and the print and multimedia publishing industries. Its special interest is the ability of SCRAN to exploit market opportunities as they arise.

The Technical Advisory Group is chaired by a very senior University figure with responsibility for Information Systems and Services and includes leading specialists and in data communications, image processing, resource discovery, interface design and virtual reality. Its special interest is SCRAN's technical viability and compliance with international standards.

The Editorial Committee is chaired by the Director of the National Museums of Scotland and includes the Historiographer Royal, the Chief Inspector of Ancient Monuments and other leading experts in history, visual arts, built heritage and museography. Its special interest is the comprehensiveness of the SCRAN resource base, the academic quality of its documentation, and its usability as a scholarly resource.

Project Closure

Many of the above quality assurance measures operate at the level of the SCRAN programme as a whole, but it will be seen that they have their effect in the validation of each of the millions of records coming in from individual projects. Only when each project's milestones have been met, all its deliverables received and checked, all corrective actions completed to an acceptable standard, and all financial statements agreed, can that project be signed off. It is moreover not until then that the final payment (usually 40 per cent of total project grant) can be made. The SCRAN approach may seem rigid and bureaucratic to some, and overly flexible to others. It is intended to be pragmatic and practical, recognizing that the final goal of Project Management is not neat and well-presented Project Plans, but successful and well-controlled Projects.

References
Books
Bradley, K,(1993) *Prince: a Practical Handbook* Oxford:

Machiavelli, N.(1514) *The Prince* Florence.

Web Sites

Morrison, I (1997) *SCRAN Basic Record Standard,* Edinburgh: http://www.scran.ac.uk/articles/basic.htm

OCLC (1999)*The Dublin Core Metadata Initiative,* Dublin Ohio. http://mirrored.ukoln.ac.uk/dc/

Turnbull, G. and Buchanan, A. (1997) *SCRAN Project Guidelines,* Edinburgh: http://www.scran.ac.uk/articles/projpaper.htm

Heritage, Scholarship and Preservation in the Digital Age

Nancy E. Elkington
Research Libraries Group
University of London Library

This paper attempts to set out some of the issues that influence us as we construct an international capacity to preserve the digital resources being created, used and re-purposed by today's scholars. It is not the aim of this symposium nor of this paper to enter into a debate on the nature of modern scholarship, on national and international notions of history, heritage and culture, nor even on collectively-acceptable definitions of primary research resources. And yet, to address the individual and organizational challenges associated with preserving today's research materials for use by tomorrow's scholars, we need to establish a common conceptual framework for thinking and talking about all of these.

Primary research resources range from cave paintings to manuscripts, from pyramids to video-tapes, from fossilized fish to printed ephemera, from botanical samples to digital satellite data. The raw materials of scholarship come in all ages, forms, sizes, compositions and conditions. They are sometimes portable, at other times stationary. They are often eye-readable but increasingly require the intervention of machines to understand and interpret. They are diverse in substance and meaning and ultimately difficult to define. All of these resources and more are nevertheless objects essential not only to the scholarly process, but also to the ability of all peoples to gain a sense of their past. Whether these resources constitute the evidence of history or heritage, of civilization or culture, are questions best left to others (Lowenthal 1999).

Research libraries, museums and archives function as collectors, keepers and, to a greater or lesser extent, interpreters of our collective cultural resources. The missions of such institutions vary in specifics, but in general they are agreed that their role is to identify, collect, preserve and make available the artifactual, intellectual and artistic products of the past and present in order that current and future generations may benefit from them. Research repositories are not exhaustive in their collecting; rather, they attempt to identify, collect and maintain a limited subset of available objects that are judged to be of contemporary and/or enduring value. Traditionally, constraints on collecting practices included relevance of material to the institution's mission, physical space limitations, budgetary restrictions on purchasing, and on the extent of available staffing to process and service the resources. Preservation activities focused on physical treatments of objects and provision of controlled storage environments to prolong their useful lives. Today, repositories face the same constraints in collecting and preserving important resources and are additionally trying to cope with the need to identify, select and preserve a deluge of electronic and digital works.

Since the advent of computer-based technologies in the middle of this century, our collective capacity to generate electronic forms of information has far outstripped our ability to manage them effectively. Information being created only in digital form is a global glut that threatens to overwhelm all of us. And yet it constitutes – in large part – the essential and ongoing evidence of our societies and institutions. Archivists, librarians and other keepers of the historic record are devising strategies and solutions they hope will be implemented in time to avoid the loss of vast amounts of digital records documenting the last half of the twentieth century.

We know that digital technology is transforming the traditional relationships between creators, publishers, keepers and users of research resources. The knowledge chain is no longer linear. It is no longer static. Interactions between links in the chain are being broken, twisted, reforged and recoupled in new and innovative ways. Today's creators of primary resources – an academic compiling field notes for an archaeological survey, a government agency capturing digital images of weather patterns on a global scale, a choreographer encoding dance movements on a laptop computer – are also behaving as small-scale publishers, using the Web as a substitute for more formally structured print resources. Publishers – creators of primary and secondary electronic sources – are struggling to define their place in a world where the scholar is less reliant on printing technologies to disseminate the results of his research. Users of online resources snap up the available digital documentary evidence to create new resources for private use and public redistribution. Libraries and archives are at once attempting to collect and preserve important digital information while at the same time becoming publishers themselves as they find new ways to make the contents of their traditional collections widely available as digital images or encoded texts on the Web. All participants in the knowledge chain are, in equal proportions, both fascinated and paralyzed by opportunities and obligations in this new digital world.

Technology captivates the imaginations of millions. Unfortunately, digital products – particularly those which are produced for individual consumption – can be an *attractive nuisance* This phrase, common in the insurance industry, is used to classify such things as swimming pools, lakes, amusement park rides and other locales that are appealing and yet dangerous to children and others lacking full powers of adult judgment. The objects so described are not, in themselves, dangerous. But they attract those who do not have the capacity to behave responsibly around them. So, too, are some digital products attractive nuisances. They are easily affordable in their most basic forms and so attract to them a range of enthusiastic adherents who know just enough to want to use them but not necessarily enough to use them wisely. As a result, keepers and preservers of digital information are sometimes hard-pressed to persuade creators that documentation, standardization and interoperability are worthy goals toward which to strive.

Researchers and other creators of primary resources often want their intellectual output to be preserved beyond their own lifetimes. In the past, it was a simple and personal matter for a scholar to collect and retain reams of notes, manuscripts, correspondence, audio tapes, printed works and data in various forms throughout his career. Toward the end of a career, the scholar or his family would decide where his unpublished life's work would be deposited. The designated library or archive organized, described and indexed the collection, placed it on the shelves and/or in boxes, and announced its availability to the community that might be supposed to have an interest in it. In turn, many of those collections would become a part of the primary resources of research for future generations. Today, the typical scholar uses computers at home, at work and in the field, saving his thoughts and analyses on a series of servers and hard drives. Some of his output is printed out and filed; most remains locked away on hard drives, perhaps occasionally backed up onto floppy disks and magnetic tape. The library or archive which accepts the deposit of such collections is faced with the onerous obligation to preserve and make the materials available. Moral, legal and financial constraints combine to make those traditional decisions and tasks difficult and often extremely expensive to carry out. Thus, the repository is immediately faced with a hard question: how much time and money should be expended to ensure that the collection (or a subset of it) survives?

Classifying the Survival of Research Resources

The survival of bio-species involves complex interplays between external physical environments, available nourishment, predators and internal adaptive skills. The survival of cultural heritage objects and research resources is no less complex and no less influenced by internal and external forces (Michalko, 1999). In broad terms, there are three means by which cultural heritage and research resources survive beyond the moment of their creation: by default, by rescue and by design.

Survival by Default

We can all think of dozens of examples of archaeological finds that have survived through centuries and millennia by default. Arrowheads, pottery shards, glass fragments, stone and bone carvings, grinding stones, baskets, bowls, jars, jewelry and hundreds of other man-made objects were made to serve an immediate need, not to survive across multiple millennia. The Tarr Steps over the River Barle, jade ornaments of ancient Chinese empires, and Neolithic cave paintings might also be classed as survivors by default, even though their creators had every reason to expect that they would last beyond a generation or two, if they thought about it at all. All of these resources have survived because, although external forces may have worked against them in their own time, internal physical stability and ongoing environmental factors worked to preserve them, if not intact, at least in situ. Modern researchers adhere to common codes of practice in investigating potential historical sites. As objects are rediscovered, great care is taken to ensure that no further damage occurs. Their locations are carefully documented, some are painstakingly removed from their resting places and handed over to professional conservators who assist in scientific investigations of the objects and also take on responsibility for ensuring their safety henceforth. The researchers and conservators work together, following common standards of practice for documenting, handling, and caring for the new-found treasures. In this way, objects that have survived by default to the end of the twentieth century stand a fair chance of surviving a good deal longer into the future, in the care of heritage agencies and research repositories.

Survival by Rescue

The Cairo Genizah, the Soviet Communist Party Archives, and the cultural heritage of Florence are just three examples of survival by rescue. The Cairo Genizah, a cache of 140,000 manuscript fragments discovered in 1898, was rescued and dispersed among a half dozen researchers around the world. Cambridge University, the largest holder of these fragments, has invested enormous amounts of time and effort to describe, transcribe, stabilize and conserve, microfilm and now digitize the fragments, some of which are up to two thousand years old. As a result, scholars around the globe have access to catalogues, reproductions and transcriptions of the original fragments. The Soviet Communist Party Archives were rescued from clear intentions of destruction because Russian archivists not only kept items they were ordered to discard, but also actively sought the means to preserve them until they could be made public. In a joint project with the Hoover Institution, millions of controversial documents are being catalogued, microfilmed and salvaged for the benefit of scholars worldwide. When the River Arno flooded in 1966, thousands of paintings, frescoes, statues, manuscripts, buildings and other cultural objects were immersed in water. And when the water receded, what remained was not only wet but covered in the mud and muck of a river in full spate. The global conservation community responded by travelling to Florence to begin the rescue operations, saving a large proportion of the damaged materials.

In each of these cases, and in the thousands of other examples that occur repeatedly around the world, a valued resource is found to be at risk of loss. Recovery procedures are often extraordinarily expensive and can take decades or centuries to complete. The common denominator in the three situations outlined above is that, in each case, the procedures developed to preserve the items meet with international standards for such work. Preservation work is undertaken by trained professionals, the work is fully documented and the copying technologies used are consistent with the best practices being followed globally. Access and preservation are linked goals, resulting in new bodies of important resources being made available to scholars everywhere.

Survival by Design

The Pyramids, the Great Wall of China and Stonehenge are three of many man-made structures that have survived because of a single, simple fact: they were designed to meet the needs of cultures which placed a high value on longevity and endurance. Constructed of durable materials to exacting specifications, some of these sites have survived even an understanding of their original purpose and use. Never exposed to overwhelming environmental forces, they survive because their internal structures are robust and because their only real predator – man – happened not to destroy them. In some cases, the sites were lost or forgotten for centuries before being rediscovered by strangers. In other cases, the site was so integral to the local cultural landscape that it was unquestioningly left to survive without additional assistance or intervention.

Magna Carta and the Declaration of Independence represent two further examples of survival by deliberate choice. Both documents were, at the time of their creation, of immense cultural value. And both documents have been perceived over time as increasingly valuable national icons. As a consequence, from the moment of their creation, they have been treated with care and maintained as the treasures they are. The Stone of Scone, while not a document, retains similar status as a national icon. Even during its 700-year absence from Scotland, it was steadfastly retained and preserved.

Protective Custody

These three survival modes alone do not tell the whole story. In fact, in each case, the objects most likely to endure will do so because they have been moved into the protective custody of a caretaking entity. This notion of protective care is not entirely new. Governments deliberately preserved the written evidence of decisions reached, laws enacted, battles engaged; the documentary evidence was systematically taken into the care of record-keepers. Museums came into their own in the nineteenth century, evolving out of a desire to give protection to historical artifacts and to provide a venue for prolonged viewing by the deeply curious. Libraries as we now know them came about through a combined desire to protect and preserve; access to them for any but a small elite is a relatively modern concept.

We selectively and insistently choose to extend the natural life of objects in which we invest great meaning and importance. The cultural resources that survive in our landscapes and repositories reflect decisions we make to ensure that internal and external stresses that might cause damage are minimized. Archaeological finds are cared for by museums where they can be stabilized, conserved, viewed and studied. Rescued documents and artifacts are deposited in libraries and archives, where they are properly protected and made available. Historic sites are often accessible but on a limited basis. These prized and protected objects and places are unique and defining records of our cultures. They survive for a variety of reasons. They endure as cultural resources when they are given protective custody.

Imagining the Future

If we accept that most traditional research resources survive beyond their time of creation either by default, through rescue efforts, or by explicit choice, and if we further agree that taking survivors into protective custody extends their useful lives, we can use this understanding to consider survival strategies in the digital age. A few brief – and only slightly imaginative – scenarios sketching some of the obstacles to effective digital preservation will perhaps serve to illustrate the kinds of challenges that creators, keepers and users of digital resources may face.

Scenario 1: The year is 2300. You are a marine biologist. Your research focus is on the spread of the global "green" movement that radically altered the way the world's water resources were managed between 1940 and 2040. Specifically, you are developing a theory to account for the huge investments in experimental, under-water cities constructed after 2050 along the East Coast of the Americas and the West Coast of Europe and Africa. You are seeking primarily government documents and data that were collected by some of the less enthusiastic nations bordering the Atlantic Ocean. Unfortunately, over 75 per cent of the machine-readable data collected by half of the nations between 1940 and the end of 1999 were lost because of complications in the computer transition to the year 2000. And, although data from the other nations exist in massive off-line data storage facilities and are theoretically alive and well, they have never been processed or indexed and so are effectively inaccessible.

Scenario 2: The year is 2200. You are an art historian. Your research focus is on the social and commercial influences that caused artists to abandon their reliance on light-lens cameras and depend instead on digital ones for still art photography in the late twentieth century. You are specifically interested in documenting the surprisingly rapid decline in the use of traditional photographic equipment and film. You want to focus on the art photographers whose livelihoods depended on a public aesthetic that embraced the digital and rejected the photographic. Large collections of original photographic prints and negatives survive from the period 1970-1990. Within these, some of the negative film has been lost due to poor storage conditions, much of the colour in transparencies and prints has shifted and faded, but most of the black and white images have survived quite well. Many of these collections were deposited in libraries and archives and were stabilized, catalogued, indexed, and properly stored. The originals survive in the hundreds of thousands. Unfortunately, nearly the entire output of the early decades of the digital movement have been lost. Some artists saved their digital output on floppy disks or wrote them to CD-ROMs, not understanding that those were not permanent storage containers.

Most of the digital master images were discarded by the artists themselves, written over, or deleted. You will not be able to carry out the kinds of extensive assessments of differing art forms that you had intended because all that survive for investigation now are the small number of digital images that were printed out and mounted for public exhibition and sale.

Scenario 3: The year is 2100. You are a cultural historian. Your research focus is on the political, educational and economic impact of popular on-line access to cultural resources. You are specifically interested in one of the first national attempts to digitize and disseminate still and moving images, text and sound that represented a centralized resource containing a wide range of cultural objects in late twentieth and early twentyfirst century Scotland. Fortunately, when the original on-line service was dismantled, all of the digital data contained in it were dispersed among a dozen different archives, libraries, and museums; since the dispersal, most of the repositories have successfully migrated the image, text and sound files onto new computing platforms. The contents of the service can be reconstructed from acquisition records at the repositories and copies of the original data can be retrieved. Because the file formats were more or less standard, most have made the transition into new storage systems without significant loss. Unfortunately, because no snapshot or other record of the actual look and feel and performance of the original service was retained, your research – as originally conceived – cannot be successfully completed.

Scenario 4: The year is 2002. You are an archaeologist. For the last five years you have collected comparative data informally from colleagues working on over two dozen Chinese sites in addition to your own field notes from a dig last year. Your files are all organized efficiently on your laptop. You have spreadsheets, Microsoft Word files, and a range of photographs and other digital images stored away. You have about 1500 emails from various colleagues around

47

the world stored and indexed in an easy-to-use database. You even maintain your personal calendar and address book in an organizer program. Your bookmarks for Web pages are well-maintained and current. This approach – keeping all your personal documents in the same place – has worked well in the past. In fact, the current laptop is your second and you had little difficulty transferring the contents of the hard drive from the previous one into your present one. But two days ago you opened an email containing a free software program. It looked interesting so you ran it. It contained a virus. It wiped out 80 per cent of the contents of your hard drive and what remains is a mess. Yesterday you called Seamus Ross to find out what to do and he gave you the names of two data recovery companies. The first thing they both asked was: When was the last time you backed up your hard drive? Your silence was sufficient response. After hearing their price estimates for recovering your data, you heaved the laptop out the nearest window and retired to the corner pub.

Some of these scenarios are admittedly a bit far-fetched (and the last one wholly imagined but not impossible to conceive). Further, they vastly underplay and oversimplify the issues that face creators of digital resources and future generations of researchers. Nevertheless, they illustrate five important points. First, that future access to digital information will require agreements and significant resource commitments from a very wide range of individuals, organizations and government agencies in which responsibility for long-term retention is vested. Second, that some data and some data characteristics will be deliberately sacrificed so that we can afford to maintain appropriate levels of access to a subset of what we think will be needed. Third, that creators and users of digital information owe it to themselves and to future generations to behave responsibly as they contribute to and make use of the growing global array of digital resources. Fourth, and perhaps the most difficult to articulate, most of us feel an instinctive compulsion to try to save as much digital information as we possibly can. This is in direct contradiction to the way we view more traditional resources, where we have long acknowledged that, not only can we not afford to preserve everything indefinitely, but no one would thank us if we did. And fifth, that the failure to move valued objects into the custody of responsible agents may guarantee that they are lost to future generations.

Preserving the Present

All of those in whom digital preservation responsibilities are vested recognize the essential fragility of digital data and the many barriers that exist to prevent digital information from surviving. They know that digital resources will only survive into the future through extraordinary rescue efforts or by design at the point of creation in combination with responsible custodial care. Librarians, archivists and information technologists around the world are working individually and collectively on the best ways to preserve digital information. They are developing technical strategies and organizational models that will enhance our ability to preserve digital information over the medium and long-term. They are also attempting to develop realistic cost models that will help to forecast more accurately the real and on-going costs of preserving very large amounts of digital information in systems that are both secure and accessible over time.

Public and private repositories have already begun to acquire, manage, preserve, and make available published and unpublished digital information that come from a range of predictable sources: individuals, educational and commercial organizations, professional associations, publishers, municipal governments/local authorities, regional/national government departments and agencies, and more. The kinds of data they are now or will soon be managing include: email, databases, spreadsheets, word-processed documents, images, sound files, financial systems, inventory/stock control systems, Web sites, office document systems, advertising/communication systems, personnel management systems, weather/climate data, census and population studies, to name but a few.

Research repositories are doing their best to act responsibly on their obligations to provide secure environments for the materials within their purview (Feeney, 1999). And, because they share a vision of what the digital future might look like, they are acting together to agree best practices, work toward international standards, and build archiving systems that are ultimately as accessible as possible. In very general terms, responsible digital archives will be designed along similar lines and will have similar attributes. Most good digital archives will have:

- A written plan which spells out and justifies the archive's assumptions and practices
- Validated procedures and capabilities against an internationally-approved implementation standards checklist
- Defined interactions between the archive staff and data providers
- A data acquisition process that can handle the expected transfer in a manner acceptable to the provider
- An accessioning process that maintains the fidelity of the original data
- Adequate environmental and disaster prevention/recovery controls
- Accepted policies and practices to periodically refresh data
- Accepted policies and practices to migrate data across media
- Accepted policies and practices to migrate data and metadata across technologies
- Appropriate and effective access to data and services by its user community(ies)
- Mechanisms and procedures for life cycle maintenance

Information specialists, archivists and librarians are working internationally to design and build technical environments, workflows and data description models; common approaches are beginning to emerge in large part because of leading edge efforts here in the United Kingdom (UK), Australia, the United States, and on the European Continent (Cedars, NEDLIB, PADI, RLG *et al.*). Individuals creating digital materials are beginning to understand that their decisions have a direct impact on whether their resources can or cannot be successfully archived. Increasingly, scholars acknowledge a range of obligations toward their data, toward those responsible for storing and providing access to digital resources, and toward future users of those resources. Some of those obligations are described briefly below.

Responsible Use of Technology

The responsible use of digital technology requires that the creator invest time and thought into what he wishes to accomplish and how the resource(s) that are produced will be used over time. First and foremost, an early assessment of long-term goals will help situate the project or initiative in a context that will rule out certain technology applications and rule in others. Following standards is almost always simpler than ignoring them. If you do not know how best to approach certain types of data, *do not guess and do not invent*. **Ask.** Take advantage of the extremely helpful specialist support services environment available, for example, to scholars in the UK through the Joint Information Systems Committee and the Research Councils.

Documentation

Whether you are collecting sampled data from field excavations, compiling sets of satellite images, re-purposing data for further use by yourself and others, or if you expect to deposit your work for archiving by a repository, you will need to document exactly how you constructed your resource. What is it? What types of files are included? What software releases were used to create them? How large are the files? How will the resource be used? Keep track of what you have done and why you designed things the way you did. When you change tack or add functionality to your files, update the documentation to keep it as current as your resource. If you are using unique or innovative applications or customized programs, these will have to be fully documented and any special hardware or software needed to use the resource will have to be defined. Better yet, use standard applications and seek advice about ways to improve functionality. And consider whether or not the original operating environment lends critical meaning to the data.

Risk Mitigation

Mechanical failures account for the greatest amount of data lost. Second in the running are viruses imported inadvertently by people hoping for a new tool or a free upgrade or simply sharing files and email across networks. Human errors also account for a percentage of the overall loss of data in the personal or home environment. Although not all major disasters or minor emergencies can be avoided, their impact on your work can be mitigated through regular and reliable backup procedures. Routine backups should be run at least weekly; if you work in a client/server environment, find out how often the systems managers backup the contents of the servers; if you work in an unsupported department or at home, backup your files onto floppies or zip floppies. The floppies should be stored at a distance from the source files. And the floppies used for backing up should be replaced regularly and checked to ensure data integrity. If you are managing your data in a Web environment, standard security controls should be in place to prevent data from being altered either accidentally or deliberately. And all documentation should be backed up and stored separately from the source files and from the backup files.

Deposit Agreements

In the UK Higher Education community there is probably already a data service for your discipline that is ready to discuss deposit arrangements with you. As a depositor, you should be aware that you will need to know a good deal about your data, and you will be expected to provide documentation regarding its creation. Further, you will need to convey enough information about any potential rights management issues (e.g., copyrights and literary property rights) pertaining to the files to enable the archive to manage the resources – and access to them – appropriately. You will need to have a sense of how often you will be updating or adding to the deposited resource. You will also be expected to communicate openly and regularly about your resource as it is being assessed and managed in the archive. As creators of digital scholarly resources in the UK, you are living the dream of academics elsewhere. The Arts and Humanities Data Service and its subject-based subsidiaries exist to help you. Take advantage of their advice, their guides to good practice and their ability to store and provide access to digital resources (Greenstein and Beagrie, 1999).

Revisiting the Future

If we return briefly to the four scenarios laid out earlier and examine a point or two from each, we can begin to clarify our thinking about what is most likely to survive and why. In each case, key actions taken or failures to act by creators and keepers of digital information resulted in the inability to identify or use the needed digital resources.

Scenario 1. The marine biologist (in 2300) cannot carry out his research because national governments failed to implement information policies that stipulated and budgeted for appropriate technical retooling to avert digital disasters, and government archives accepted the deposit of materials that they could not afford to make accessible. Further, the archives decided to move unprocessed and unindexed data to off-line storage systems in the hope that someday they would be able to afford to process them properly. Nearly three hundred years later, the data sit, possibly intact, but inaccessible. Although this scenario is overly pessimistic, it is not outside the bounds of possibility. The good news is twofold. First, some national archives (including the Public Record Office) have begun to work with the departments and agencies that are creating digital information to ensure that what is eventually moved into the care of the archive is actually archivable. And second, an international federation of government archives has begun working together in the InterPares project, giving particular attention to managing massive numbers of electronic records. International standards are now being developed that will eventually underpin the decisions and archiving systems on which we increasingly rely. But even with a foundation of common standards, national governments will have to finance these massive new resources. They will not be able to preserve all digital data. There is simply too much. But they will attempt to save portions of the data for current and future use.

Scenario 2. The art historian (in 2200) is also unable to pursue his research. He is attempting to trace evidence of a rapid cultural shift in the use of technology and is at the mercy of contemporary judgments by creators as to the long-term value of their own materials. Part of the difficulty is that the artists, having completed a work and produced a version for exhibition, were no longer all that interested in the component digital files. Further, they believed that their storage techniques were adequate for their needs. As they no doubt were. But were they thinking about who would have access to their digital files hundreds of years later? Probably not. If they had been, would they have been willing to save versions of digital images that they felt were unsuccessful as well as the final master images? Unlikely. If some had opportunities to deposit their digital works with a responsible archive would they have done so? In the UK, at least the option is available. Artists elsewhere in the world are not nearly so lucky. At best, a few may discover that museums or professional associations or art collectives are beginning to provide such services or at least offer sound technical advice on how to manage their digital corpus. At worst, future generations will be unable to piece together the fabric of artistic creativity in the digital age.

Scenario 3. The cultural historian (in 2100) wants a lot. In the first instance, he wants access to all of the original digital holdings of an on-line, interactive service designed to meet the needs of children, scholars and life-long learners. Well, as it turns out, the service was managed responsibly, and when it shut down it ensured that the contents were relayed to digital repositories that would preserve and maintain them securely and accessibly. But our historian is not so much interested in the individual contents as he is in the dynamic nature of the interface, the look and feel of the service at different stages of its development. Can dynamic data be preserved? The answer appears to be yes, although a good deal more work needs to be done to feel confident about this. The real challenge will be one centering on cost. How often will we be able to afford to invest in preserving the interactive nature of digital services, products, programs and Web sites? Two current research projects (at the Koninklijke Bibliothek and between the UK CEDARS project and the University of Michigan) are beginning to explore the organizational and financial implications for emulating software environments in order that dynamic information can be preserved (Rothenberg, 1998). For some time to come we will probably choose to preserve the static data that underlie the dynamic services rather than the look and feel of them, simply because it will be easier and cheaper to do so.

Scenario 4. The archaeologist (in 2002), like most of us, is more of an optimist than a realist. We go along, creating the intricate and interwoven fabric of our digital lives, without recognizing that the machines and software we are using are very fragile indeed. Could the contents of his hard drive be rescued and reconstructed? Possibly. Could he have afforded the cost? Perhaps, although it might be high and there is no advance guarantee that the salvage technicians will be able to save it all. Survival, even into the next few years, depends on more of us taking responsibility for those portions of the digital resource that we actively create and control. That means backing up, upgrading software programs, migrating databases, and seeking expert advice before disaster happens (Ross & Gow 1999).

Closing Remarks

We are undoubtedly in a period of transition. In this last half of the twentieth century we have seen digital technology revolutionize data processing in all its forms; audio recording, imaging, communications, and information dissemination are just a few of the familiar forms that have been utterly transformed. Industrial, educational, cultural and consumer applications abound, leaving behind a rich but massive body of digital data. The bits and bytes representing our cultural heritage are literally everywhere. At the same time, cultural institutions and agencies are building a global capacity to cope with a range of new digital preservation activities. Within the next decade, we should see the deployment of trusted archiving systems around the world. But we are not there yet. Very little has made its way into trusted archiving systems because very few such systems exist. Much work remains to be done, and librarians, archivists and information specialists are doing their part.

Every positive action taken by creators of digital resources today will increase the likelihood that data may survive into the future. Doing nothing will almost certainly guarantee that data will end up in a digital diaspora. A digital diaspora is the not-so-distant circumstance when disassociated, undocumented, non-standard and dispersed data survive, perhaps, but in forms and in places which are inaccessible. No one knows the data resource exists, so no one can ask to see or use it. The fact is that, with the best will in the world, we cannot preserve everything. We never could, nor have we ever tried to do so. The sheer volume of data now being produced is on a scale that defies any sensible plan to preserve it all. Even preserving a subset will be a financial burden of huge proportions. We must therefore be both highly selective and forward-thinking as we create and preserve new resources.

Survival by design in the digital age means advance planning by creators and keepers. It means partnerships among all the links in the knowledge chain and all the players on the cultural heritage field.

We should be constructing resources that are preservable at a reasonable cost and selecting only those for long-term retention that we think will be most needed in future. We must act responsibly – individually and collectively – on the data that are designated for long-term retention. Creating, using and preserving digital cultural resources is both a challenge and a privilege. As we share that privilege, we owe it to our future colleagues to meet the challenge and to rise to it together. Anything less would be irresponsible.

References
Books
Feeney, M. (1999) (editor) D*igital Culture. Maximising the Nation's Investment,* National Preservation Office, London.

Michalko, J. (forthcoming) Equilibrium and opportunism. Information strategies and the new environment, *New Library World.*

Web Sites
Cedars – CURL Exemplars in Digital Archives – UK project among members of the Consortium of University Research Libraries to develop a cooperative digital archive **(http://www.leeds.ac.uk/cedars/)**.

Greenstein, D. and Beagrie, N. (1999) Arts and Humanities Data Service Web site, including: "Creating a Viable Scholarly Data Resource" **(http://ahds.ac.uk/deposit/viable.html)**, "Guides to Good Practice" **(http://ahds.ac.uk/public/guides.html)**, "Managing Digital Collections: AHDS Policies, Standards, and Practices" **(http://ahds.ac.uk/public/srg.html)**, "Digital Preservation: a Guide to Web Resources" **(http://ahds.ac.uk/resource/preserve.html)**, "Rights Management Framework" **(http://ahds.ac.uk/bkgd/rmf1.htm)**, "Depositing Data with the AHDS" **(http://ahds.ac.uk/deposit/depintro.html)**, and "Copyright FAQ" **(http://ahds.ac.uk/copyrightfaq.html)**, among others. Also "Draft Joint C&IT Policy" with the Arts and Humanities **Research Board (http://www.ahrb.ac.uk/citpol.html)**.

NEDLIB – National Electronic Deposit Library – EU-funded project to develop a European library of digital documents in a stable archival environment (http://www.kb.nl/coop/nedlib/index.html)

PADI – Preserving Access to Digital Information – Web site of digital preservation projects and information managed by the National Library of Australia (http://www.nla.gov.au/padi/about.html).

Research Libraries Group Web site, including: Hedstrom, M and Montgomery, S (1999) *Digital Preservation Needs and Requirements in RLG Member Institutions* (http://www.rlg.org/preserv/digpres.html).

Ross, S. and Gow, A. (1999) *Digital Archaeology: The Recovery of Digital Materials at Risk*, British Library Research and Innovation Centre, Report 108, London.

Rothenberg, J. (1998) *Avoiding Technological Quicksand: Finding a Viable Technical Foundation for Digital Preservation*, Council on Library and Information Resources, Washington, DC. Also available at: http://www.clir.org/pubs/reports/rothenberg/contents.html

Enhancing Access, Ensuring Services: Data in the Digital Library

Peter Burnhill
EDINA National Data Centre
Edinburgh

Introduction

The purpose of this paper is to examine how to enhance access to scholarly resources, supposing that the arrival of the digital age might provide the key to unlock this Nation's riches. Part of the answer may lie in an assessment of the impact that the digital age has had and is having on scholarly activity. However, there is a call to do more than that: It no longer suffices to ask what effect will the Internet have on ...? Rather, we must comprehend the institutional world from which the Internet arose, and the many and various worlds with which the Internet now coevolves, and make sense of the technology in that dynamic context.' (Agre, 1998)

If this argument is persuasive then we have a broad canvas: we might have to take as context how we view the culture of scholarship and the role of its institutions and of intermediaries, perhaps having special regard to the universities and their political economy. The latter regard would include both the internal information economy required to sustain scholarly activity and its relation to the worlds of international electronic commerce and, nearer to home, the wider agenda of government, including the new institutions of governance within Scotland. More concretely, the objective of enhanced access to resources of scholarly data, requires services as well as resources that will endure. Inevitably reference must be made to the concept of the digital library. Given the limited way in which this is presently implemented in libraries, this is also an opportunity to put matters to do with data to the fore - to put data into the digital library. In scholarship, data are not just digital, they have meaning as evidence.

For this paper I have drawn on assorted experience in helping to develop university-based data libraries. I should disclose my occupational and disciplinary perspective. This was initially that of a social scientist and statistician, generating survey data of school leavers in Scotland for others to analyze. This then broadened to numeric data files produced by government, commerce as well as by academic research groups. For that I should also acknowledge debt to members of the International Association of Social Science Information Service and Technology (IASSIST) who have helped me over the past fifteen years. As current President of IASSIST, one of my responsibilities is to promote that international group for data archivists, data librarians and others who work in this area (http://datalib.library.ualberta.ca/iassist/). My work over the past five years has been to establish the EDINA national data centre, and this has widened my perspective. EDINA provides tertiary education in the United Kingdom (UK) with on-line access services to bibliographic facilities as well as to research data that can range from historical texts to digital mapping; further information is found at http://edina.ac.uk/. EDINA is one of three UK datacentres, that are among a much larger array of services that provide the Distributed National Electronic Resource (DNER); further references are found at http://www.jisc.ac.uk/.

This paper begins with a review of what is different about digital resources and of what resources to regard as scholarly, and comments on the differing traditions we might draw upon in developing services to provide access to documents and data. There is a special regard for the role of institutions and for scholarly resources on and about the people of Scotland. The latter are included to prompt discussion with policy-makers about an appropriate forum at which to devise policy and allocate resources to provide Scotland with its digital library.

In the Digital Age
At the dawn of the digital age we may not be able to judge so very

much. There is rapid change and the new is soon take for granted: email has been a given for many years; access to material on the World Wide Web by academic staff and students is now presumed. But we also know that words, number, pictures, sounds all shall and will be digital, and accessed from afar. Much of this will be commonplace.

I suggest that there are three essential differences about digital resources. First, because the information objects are digital, they can be copied, re-formatted, combined with one another and distributed with ease that was not possible hitherto. With the shift from the physical to the digital, the concept of an original digital work is less appropriate: all are copies, even those designated as back-up, and archival copies in another sense. What is important is the relation between the digital work and the work it re-presents. Usage, per se, does not diminish the object; the concept of wear and tear is re-defined to relate instead to the properties of the media that hold the object. There is no physical or inherent scarcity, nor any inherent queue. Digital information objects can be disseminated in any manner of variously sized digital buckets on magnetic tape, (floppy) diskette, compact disk (CD), cartridge and the like.

Second, digital objects can be subjected to manipulation for many purposes, and in ways not previously possible with physical media, including selective retrieval, analysis and display. To carry out these operations we require software. Software is capitalized skill, the digital embodiment of methods and techniques that are developed by a person or group in one place and time, and available for others to use at another place and another time. Among the most significant set of algorithms and methods for the present discussion are those associated with the database, both databases which act as host to the digital information objects and those in which information about these objects is held and accessed. The latter information is referred to as metadata.

Third, the carrier that allows transport of the object is also now digital. Telecommunication networks mean that users can disregard distance. Digital networks provide increases in the speed and volume of traffic that allow information objects to be accessed in what can seem to us to be instant: at the same time although at a different place. The client/server model developed across these networks means that data can be accessed from several different remote servers, processed on a further server and displayed on one's (client) desktop, as though in one action. Increases in bandwidth, more advanced use of transport protocols and clever software have allowed us to move from the discrete activities of access and dissemination by remote log-on, file transfer and email communication, to have the opportunity to maintain a session and present material through the interactive use of text, voice and video. We can, as indicated, join up a series of activities, variously termed interconnectivity or interoperability.

These differences, of object, of operators and of transport, radically change the economics and the geography of access and use. Those who wish to use a resource need not be in the same place as the resource and, in theory at least; the resource can be accessed at any time. The World Wide Web became significant so quickly, not because it represented a technological breakthrough (it did not), but because it demands little from the user. It soon became the de facto arena for interaction. This shift in thinking about access is reflected in thinking about libraries: from access to places, where the library is defined as a building and physical collection, to access within spaces, where the library is regarded as a manager of digital information spaces (Dempsey 1998 pp. 234-41).

This brief overview must be qualified. First, although in the preceding paragraphs the term data could be used instead of the phrase digital objects, this would risk confusion as the term data has a specialized use in scholarship. What is made digital data may also be regarded as empirical data, available as evidence and for analysis.

Similarly, the availability of commercial software, and of desktop computers, may have impact on the work of scholars as it does of other white-collar workers. However, in scholarship, software has been used to embody, and share, methods that are devised for various aspects of scholarly activity, especially in empirically-based explanation.

Scholarly Resources

What is scholarly about resources? Scholarly resources do not exist: the scholarly process defines them. Three categories of scholarly resources can be identified: those that are scholarly by prior design; those that are defined to be scholarly by post hoc, archival designation; and those that form part of scholarly communication.

In the first category, scholarly by prior design, the resources are created as part of investigations, as part of activity carried out by or on behalf of scholars. Classically, these resources are data to be used as evidence to support empirical statements. For this purpose, they are defined to exist as data by (prior) theory and generated by use of some form of instrumentation. Examples include data constructed by the astronomer recording observations by telescope, the naturalist recording habitat and patterns of behaviour, the social scientist recording answers to questionnaire; the historian extracting records from archives. In recent times these resources are increasingly, now almost universally, data in the sense of being digital through various techniques of data capture. As the research process has become automated, so scholarly resources are born digital.

What is problematic in this argument is whether these resources are really regarded by their creators as a product for others to use, or only as a by-product of their particular research project. Are they monopoly working capital to be used-up and discarded, or are they assets to be taken forward and transformed for re-use? Who should carry out the appraisal, and to what effect?

The second category of scholarly resource, those that are defined to be scholarly by post hoc, archival designation, describes many of resources that we call scholarly, and include many reported as the projects in this volume. These resources were initially brought into existence by processes and for purposes other than that of scholarship. Other examples would include everyday cultural items, ranging from pots to bus tickets to specific contemporary records. They become scholarly when they are used for scholarly purpose or, in advance of need, were identified by archival appraisal as having potential use for scholarly purpose. However, the projects reported in this volume often report more than just the production of digital surrogates. We should regard the databases of descriptive comment and metadata that have been created to enhance the means to access the digital surrogates as scholarly data resources that count in our first category, those that are scholarly by prior design.

This brings us to scholarly communication as a third category of scholarly resource. Scholarly communication is the dissemination of the results of scholarly activity. These are summary statements made about the social, physical or intellectual world, in the language of systematic theory. The relation between research activity and research publication is complex (Burnhill and Tubby-Hille, 1994). In general, finished work is demonstrated as formal publication: as articles in peer-reviewed journals or as book-length monographs - the choice dependent upon disciplinary tradition. For example, published work is both container for research results (boxes for the fruits of scholarly work) and scholarly statement. But such published work is generally regarded as scholarly communication only if it provides information about method and reference to some scholarly resource, according to some notion of reproducibility. Scholarly communication should therefore include the citation of scholarly data resources. Although it can be argued that these communications are themselves scholarly resources, as they are re-used by others for scholarly purposes, they are not the main focus of our attention here. They are mentioned both for completeness, and also because there are observations to be made on the accessibility of this material and on organizational change as all becomes digital.

Both journal articles and monographs are created and are becoming available in digital format, just as the bibliographic finding aids, such as on-line library catalogues of holdings and the databases of abstracts and specialist indexing, have been for over ten years. The academic journal market forms part of a larger market that is itself in a state of flux in a relatively minor sector of the burgeoning information economy; commercial imperatives and scholarly concerns clash.

The traditional value chain is being challenged. The author and the reader were not previously in direct contact, except in the discrete arena of academic conference and seminar. As part of the formal act of dissemination, the author provided the finished work to the publishing house, which might use peer review or special editors but would in any event prepare the work for others to use, as part of their publication and distribution activities. The reader, on the other hand, would go either to a library or to a bookshop. Subscription agents played the role of go-between for the many publishers and the many libraries and booksellers. The middle is now being squeezed in ways that are providing a challenge to (copy) rights and the conventions of publishing.

First, various types of electronic intermediary are emerging, but it is those organizations that control the rights to content, including the abstract and index databases but mainly the whole text of articles, that have been transforming themselves into the front-line providers of on-line services. Second, dissemination of finished work can be achieved by authors less through distribution by 'publishers', than by providing the means of access to pre-prints across the Internet. There is no apparent need for the intermediary. However, few authors make good publishers, or good librarians; nor should they be required to play such roles. There is a risk that the access may not be of long-standing, that a work of potential scholarly value comes to be like the grey literature of working papers.

The properties of digital objects, software and network connectivity have allowed linkage of activities. This is having an effect upon the accessibility of the scholarly data resources as with scholarly communication. First, it is possible to generalize from the prospect of easy linkage between discovering a journal article of interest and the subsequent access to the article itself.

Second, the prospect of interconnectivity blurs the distinction between scholarly results and scholarly resources. Readers of scholarly statement are provided with easier means with which to contest the empirical evidence in scholarly statement. As the cost of distribution no longer inhibits 'publication', there is prospect that the grey literature describing the encoding of data might also be read on-line. But some scholarly reward should exist for such 'publication'. What of the digital resources that are cited: should the work that led to their creation, publication and availability also be recognized for scholarly reward? If that is the intent, what arrangements exist for peer review?

Information, Document or Data

When thinking how to be practical, implementing services to deliver online access to scholarly resources, for example, it can be useful to find some theoretical basis. For this we should be able to turn to scholars who work in information studies or information science. Searching on the Web, I found a preprint of an article by Michael Buckland (1999), who as President of the American Society of Information Science, discusses the history of his subject:

'Although it is a considerable simplification, I think that it can be helpful to think in terms of two traditions, or mentalities, even cultures, that co-exist in the area of Information Science: (i) Approaches based on a concern with documents, with signifying records: archives, bibliography,

documentation, librarianship, records management, and the like; and (ii) approaches based on finding uses for formal techniques, whether mechanical (such as punch cards and data-processing equipment) or mathematical (as in algorithmic procedures).' (Buckland, 1999).

Buckland sees these as complementary, but non-convergent traditions. The latest project is to build the digital library, an ambiguous phrase which describes both the modernization of library services and the infrastructure to provide access to complex databases; a strange admixture of the two traditions. Developments in the name of the digital library are prompting re-examination of many of the principles thought to underlie the practices in the dissemination, access and presentation developed for pre-digital documents, especially so on (metadata) standards for description.

There is a third tradition, of secondary analysis. As indicated, data can also mean evidence. Seeking empirically based explanation, social science researchers required access to computer-readable resources generated by others. This prompted the growth of a hybrid culture of data librarians and data archivists whose aim was to provide long-run shared access to what were first called machine-readable data files. The international association to which I referred earlier, IASSIST, is now over twenty-five years old, and brings together a wide variety of professionals, in the universities, national statistics offices, national records archives and more, who work to make social science data files accessible and who work with what they call data producers.

Questions and Verbs

The approach taken here comes from this third tradition, of secondary analysis. What should we expect of a library of scholarly data resources? I was faced with a similar question in 1984, when establishing a data library for use by staff and students in the Universities of Edinburgh, Glasgow and Strathclyde across the wide area network then supported by the Regional Computing Organisation Network. I had to consider what a data library was or could become and wrote a paper that was later presented to the Committee of Librarians and Statisticians in the UK and to a working party convened by the National Science Foundation in the United States and the Economic and Social Science Research Council. This paper considered the matter from the point of view of a researcher, in twelve problem-focussed questions:

1. Is the problem in hand likely to benefit from empirical evidence?
2. Are there data available that could shed light on this problem?
3. Where is the database located?
4. How may I negotiate access?
5. What are the provenance, status and quality of the data?
6. Can I obtain codebooks and allied documentation?
7. How may I re-cast my problem so that these data can contribute?
8. What software is available for data retrieval, re-coding, analysis and presentation?
9. Will the data, the documentation and software permit me to assess accuracy and reliability?
10. Can I use this software myself?
11. How may I obtain hard copy of the results from the analysis?
12. What will be the cost in time and money?
    (Burnhill 1985 p3).

These are questions that potential users of a scholarly data resource might still ask. The first question would prompt the review of what was a scholarly resource. The next three questions have been simplified into three verbs: 'discover, locate, request'. Together with "access", these form the four demand-side verbs that were derived in the MODELS workshops run during the past four years as part of the Joint Information Systems Committee (JISC)'s eLib

Programme. MODELS is an acronym for MOving to Distributed Environments for Library Services, http://www.ukoln.ac.uk/.

The focus is now on Internet resources, on how to help the potential user discover material of interest given the great increase in both the number of potentially relevant scholarly data resources, especially given the even greater number of other irrelevant material. The problem of discovery, however, is of long standing. Those who worked in what used to be called the statistical reference section of research libraries would ask: 'as major uncertainty haunts the user when a desired piece of statistical information is not found..Was this because it does not exist, or because the source was not discovered?' (Hamilton, 1982). That problem still remains, and will grow as more scholarly resources are made available in digital form online.

The problem facing users on how to discover what resources exists is one of the main driving forces in the construction of the digital library, and in the UK, of the Distributed National Electronic Resource. It has given rise to a number of what are termed resource discovery services. In particular, there is a Resource Discovery Network (RDN) organized on a subject basis, with six Faculty Hubs. These supercede and incorporate earlier subject gateways.

From the perspective of those who create or make available scholarly data resources, the equivalent supply-side questions are to do with how to be noticed. Search mechanisms for resource discovery are heavily dependent upon the creation and accessibility of structured metadata that describe digital information objects and collections. The services that support access need to provide that metadata if they wish their collections to be noticed. It is here that the first two traditions in Information Science may conflict. On the one hand there is an attempt to construct the latter-day version of the Abstract and Indexing databases used for journal articles. On the other hand, that effort competes with the blunderbuss of the commercially-available search engines and search robots, which combine the advantages of free-text searching with algorithms for advanced automated classification.

Sometimes discovering the existence of what you seek also amounts to finding it. Other times it does not. You have the reference but do not know where it may be located. The location of organizations that can offer services on the object of interest is the next step for the potential user. However, it is important not to conflate the problem of identification with the related, but separate problem of location. Because a scholarly resource is in digital format, this means that there is no unique copy. There can be more than one copy, located and accessible from more than one place. Moreover, there can be different editions, or versions. A system of identifiers and authority files is required. With changes in the definition of seriality, it may be that we can adopt the system used for in the International Standard Serials Number (ISSN) for larger purpose. What are also required are services that can match identifiers of information objects to the location of services being offered on those objects.

Next is the matter of negotiating access, at question 4 - the MODELS verb is 'request'. The aim is to provide access to data resources for scholarly purposes. We can view this as a matter of privilege or payment; of membership or money; of library card or debit card. The principle that access should be free at the point of use was successfully asserted and maintained through the strident political years of market economics in the face of the claim that the end user should pay. The privilege of access may depend on who the potential user is and the potential usage to which the resources are to be put. Privilege depends upon membership. Attention is now on services enabling authorization of access that are based on institutional membership. There are also classic problems of 'externalities' in this information economy for scholarship. The bulk of the costs to create a data resource, or to provide services for access, are sunk costs. The marginal costs of providing access, as of electronic distribution, are very small; but even marginal cost pricing does not balance the books.

The supply-side equivalent to this question is to do with who can make the offer to meet the request. This is about rights management, a topic with far-reaching implications, as the whole field of rights management is undergoing major change in order to support electronic commerce. The most interesting place to start to find out more about this field is the INDECS Project, http://www.indecs.org/.

There is an internal economy for scholarship that we must strive to protect. The reward structure for scholarly activity is recognition of ideas and the opportunity to command resources to put these to the test. The consideration for use of another's resource in scholarship, be these ideas or results, is in the form of acknowledgment through citation. However, with data, it is most often the case that one wants to do more than view or copy an extract. The reason for wanting to access scholarly resources in digital form is to manipulate their content, to combine them with other resources and to add value prior to their analysis and re-display. And arrangement must be made for others to share the benefits of that additional work. Additional rights are required for re-distribution. It is nevertheless possible to agree terms and conditions with rights holders that allow uses of data for scholarly purposes. This has been achieved with a range of organizations that were formerly very protective of copyright and which place strict limitation on re-distribution, for example, the Ordnance Survey in Great Britain.

Questions 5, 6 and 9 are collectively about documentation. They continue to be significant questions when considering access to all but the most self-descriptive of scholarly data resources. It is this aspect of the secondary analysis tradition that highlights what I see as essentially different about data in the digital library: re-use and re-usability. There may be metadata provided, for the purpose of assisting discovery and location, on what a particular information object is about, but this is more than that. Researchers who wish to re-use data in their analyses, and to apply appropriate methods, need to know how data came about, as well as what they purport to be about. Providing access to data without access to associated documentation is worse than useless, it can mislead. There are strong arguments that the documentation ought to be at least as accessible as the resource that it describes.

Questions 8 and 11 are ones of logistics, but matters to do with the availability of software are germane for both the potential user, and the institution to which he or she belongs, and to the agency that provides access to the scholarly resource. The focus here has been on scholarly data resources, but access to scholarly software resources must also have a priority. For many large-scale databases, access to scholarly resource should be presented together with the opportunity to use software that manipulates and analyses as well as extracts and downloads.

Questions 7, 9 and 10 touch on matters of skill. Like the issue of rights management, this is a topic with far-reaching implications, and should merit more attention than can be given here.

The last question, question 12, concerning the cost in time and money, is a reminder that the purpose of providing access to scholarly data resources is to enhance the productivity of researchers, students and teachers in their scholarly activity.

Viability, Institutions and Services

This user-based approached is valuable but it presumes that all will continue to be well. We wish to enhance access but we also wish to ensure the prospect of future access. A basic step is to ensure the viability of a scholarly data resource. Arguments for this are provided in other papers in this symposium. A viable scholarly data resource is defined there as one that remains accessible without much (ideally without any) loss in information content despite changes in hardware, software or network technologies (AHDS, 1998).

I have argued that the prime motivation for creating scholarly resources in digital format, whether as digital surrogate or as database to facilitate use, is ease of use for the primary analyst. There is then opportunity for re-use. However, for re-use to become a reality, there is need for policy agreement and compliance on how archival responsibility is to be exercised. A statement about "archival responsibility" should be included among the fields of metadata description for an object.

What is required is both conscious decision and investment of effort, and therefore expense. This is brought about by scholarly pressure or through conditions made by funding bodies. For example, the Economic and Social Research Council has included conditions in the grants it awards about deposit of data with the Data Archive at the University of Essex. Although it is preferable that this is carried out at an early stage in the life cycle, this is a demanding expectation of a research investigator. It will be interesting to see what developments occur in respect of funded research in the arts and humanities. If creators of data seek assistance to ensure viability and therefore long term accessibility, to whom should they turn? Are these the same organizations that provide the access services?

Scholarly data resources may be created as projects, and these resources may be successfully made viable, but services are required to ensure continued access. When considering long-term accessibility, we turn to institutions that endure. Examples from each category of scholarly data resource considered here are being maintained as collections for subsequent use in scholarly purpose within the libraries, museums and archival institutions represented at this Symposium. Many of these form part of the institutional framework of universities, but many keepers of scholarly (data) resources do not; they constitute national and civic institutions.

The document tradition offers enduring principles that provide common purpose. On behalf of a relatively recent institution, a former Chairman of the Governors of the British Library wrote:

"At the end of the 20th century the principal tasks of acquisition, preservation and access [that define our role] remain fundamentally unaltered: but their scope is expanding and methods of fulfilling them are multiplying." (Kenny, 1998, p. 5)

Activity about particular scholarly resources can lay the basis for organizations. This is not new. Some may even become institutions that endure, ensuring long-term access to materials. One instance close at hand was the bequest of a collection of manuscripts and early printed material that belonged to an Edinburgh advocate, Clement Little, in legacie to the toun of Edinburgh (Kirk, pp. 20-2). The activity about that bequest is regarded as the critical beginning to what eventually became Edinburgh University Library and the University of Edinburgh.

More recent is the substantial activity generated about SCRAN, the Scottish Cultural Resource Access Network. There is evidence at this Symposium, and at its Web site (http://www.scran.org/) of the part it has played in funding digitization projects, in setting standards to assist the exercise of archival responsibility, and also in providing means of on-line access.

The Data Library at the University of Edinburgh came about in order to provide technical support to projects that involved the analysis of two related sets of large-scale data in the form of statistical summaries for mall areas from the 1971 Population Census for Scotland and from the annual Agricultural Censuses of both England and Wales and Scotland). This is now the institutional home for EDINA.

There are other, yet more recent organizations emerging, particularly university-based organizations that are playing a part in the making of the distributed national electronic resource (DNER). It is not clear how they will fare in even the medium term; and if they do survive whether they will become new institutions of long standing or adjuncts of existing institutions.

The Arts and Humanities Data Service began as an experiment to understand how specialist data services might work together through an AHDS Executive. There are five such specialist data services coordinated by the AHDS: the Archaeological Data Service, the History Data Service, the Oxford Text Archive, the Performing Arts Data Service and the Visual Arts Data Service. The development of the distributed national electronic resource is predicated on such ideas. In some respects, EDINA may have been the last of the old-style, multi-subject data centres to be created. There is a rational balance to be found, of subject expertise and technical capacity. What is important is that a sensible division of labour is arrived at, both among the university-based data services and with other keepers of scholarly data resources. The latter includes universities, their departments and scholars; national, civic and specialist "memory" institutions; and other not-for-profit organisations.

Accessibility is one of the keywords used to guide EDINA in its delivery of its online services, so too are inter-working and interoperability. Inter-working with other services is very important, including those that are specialist in function or subject matter. Inter-operability is a term to describe the technical underpinning that exploits the client/server model and enhances accessibility. One illustration is the way in which the EDINA Digimap service might be used. This provides the UK academic community with online access to Ordnance Survey digital mapping. Through inter-operability, EDINA might act as a map server to provide another service, the Archaeological Data Service, for example, with the option to enhance its own service with map backgrounds to geo-referenced data. A comparable example could be given with respect to the UKBORDERS service on digitized boundaries and their use with the Census Dissemination Unit or the History Data Service. There are both technical and organizational challenges but this collaboration will greatly enhance accessibility for users of scholarly data resources.

A Digital Library for the Nation's Riches

The riches in focus have been those associated with scholarly purpose. The qualifier is that of Nation, to place a focus on Scotland's riches, especially on scholarly data resources about the land and people of Scotland. More generally, there is need for a policy framework to resolve what is to be done and by whom. Not only is the technology changing rapidly. The earlier creation of the Scottish Higher Education Funding Council, and now the Scottish Parliament and its Executive, suggest changes in responsibility and opportunity, as is also suggested by the setting up of ministerial taskforce for Digital Scotland.

During the past ten years, an infrastructure for information-related services and a policy infrastructure for specialist and bibliographic datasets have been developed at the UK level. This is now largely exercised by the Joint Information Services Committee (JISC) of the higher education funding bodies, including that of Scottish Higher Education Funding Council (SHEFC). Scots have not been without influence in those UK-level developments. In particular, Michael Anderson and Derek Law were two of the most influential shapers of UK-level policy over the period, as was Sir John Arbuthnott, the former chairman of the JISC. He put the seal of approval on the launch of EDINA as a third JISC-designated national datacentres, based at the University of Edinburgh, the other two, BIDS and MIMAS, being based in England, at the Universities of Bath and Manchester, respectively.

It can be argued that scholarship within Scotland benefits from this UK framework, especially with the availability of so many sources of funding at the UK level. There is also opportunity to develop the technical infrastructure which provides the connectivity. For example, additional funding from SHEFC has assisted the development of the Metropolitan Area Networks (MANs) which provide high-speed links across Scotland. It is understood that there is to be a comparable focus by a Task Force set up by the Scottish Executive to look at creating a single broad band network for the entire public sector in Scotland, as part of Digital Scotland.

What may be required, however, is policy to guide the provision of content and of associated data services, and an on-line gateway providing pointers to existing network-accessible data sources on the Land and People of Scotland. The Scottish Confederation of University and Research Libraries (SCURL) has launched a Scottish Datasets Initiative in order to identify material relevant to the study of the land and people of Scotland, and to promote the digitization of key resources. One resource identified was the first two Statistical Accounts of Scotland, circa 1790 and circa 1840, which were subsequently digitized as page images as part of a project put forward by the University of Glasgow to the JISC. They are shortly to be made accessible as an EDINA on-line service.

There is obvious scope for inter-working, and for inter-operability within Scotland. How should we proceed? Should we move towards the creation of a Scottish Universities and Research Data Service? Acronyms abound, especially in the library and computing fields, and especially in Scotland; there is risk of irony in seeking well-articulated rationality though an organization named SURDS. Notwithstanding, more than a single Scottish Data Centre may be required to achieve institutional consensus on the division of labour about who should do what, and the structure of policy, funding and accountability. There is opportunity, and requirement, in support of scholarship, to bring into play contributions from the variety of university and research-focussed organizations, each having differing and complementary strengths.

Conclusion

There is much uncertainty about the medium-term benefits of communication and information technologies (C & IT), and more yet about what changes they will bring to our everyday lives. I like to think that the application of the digital, or C & IT technologies, is like the application of electricity during the first half of this Century. At first, existing practices were automated, then new ways of doing things were discovered, and innovative attempt made at improving productivity and overall effectiveness. If that were true, what should we expect for scholarship?

Of course, what seems important now may not be so when seen with benefit of the hindsight of even five years or less. Forecasting is difficult, especially so when the only constant seems to be change, if you will forgive the hackneyed phrase. But then I am reminded of the hackneyed phrase of the moment, the Millennium Bug, present-day hindsight on the planning horizon of system designers, programmers and those who commissioned their work. Soon we shall discover whether our post hoc appraisal was sufficient.

The universities have responsibility, at least, for appraisal of their own waste product. The scholarly research process in Scotland generates vast quantities of data as by-products. What guidance and priority should we give about what should be kept? This is not fanciful. Records of pollen count recorded in the first part of this century became the subject of so-called data archaeology to support contemporary investigation into global climate change, every bit as important as, and requiring skills comparable to, the study of mortality and fertility from nineteenth century parish registers.

The prospect of connectivity between related scholarly data resources, together with increases in ease of use, suggest considerable economic and quality advantages to be had in value-added activity: combining data derived from different sources and located in different places; and offering multiple views onto the same, often complex database of information. However, the design of user interfaces, which can prompt others to comprehend what is on offer, continues to represent a considerable challenge. Presentation, as ever, is everything if the different and varied 'publics' of research, learning and teaching are each to have a coherent view. In the absence of publishers for scholarly data resources, we need to mimic their marketing departments, or at least reflect upon the activities within and between our academic disciplines. Consider the role of the scholarly journal as an arena in which scholars communicate, as ways of defining the boundaries of disciplines, both extant and emergent. The activity to create subject-based gateways to assist in the selection of, as well as access to, resources on the Internet, and the even more recent term subject portals, are attempts to recognize, or to create, virtual communities that are the latter-day equivalent of the invisible college.

The challenge by Phillip Agre which opened this paper risked final resort to the broad canvas of the culture of scholarship and the role of its institutions, with special regard to the universities and their political economy. We need to identify what may persist and what is transient, even if profound in its impact. The Internet and the World Wide Web may turn out to be transient. Do we expect the universities to persist as enduring institutions for much that we associate with scholarly matters? Their autonomy of action has financial and hence political limits, but that is not new. What may be new, however, is the manner in which government and commerce are embracing the C & IT tools that we have been using for our trade. The means to achieve our ends may depend on how the universities meet government expectation that access to resources is widened to serve the wider agenda of life-long learning and the transformation to a knowledge-based economy. In Scotland, the universities must resolve these questions at several levels of civic government: the city, Scotland, the UK and the European Union. Within this context, we seek to provide the means to access to scholarly data resources according to the universal and international characteristics of both university scholarship, and the Internet.

References

References to a Web site are indicated by an asterisk

*Agre, P (1992) Yesterdays Tomorrow, Times Literary Supplement, 3 July 1998 (This and related articles also found at **http://dlis.gseis.ucla.edu/people/pagre/.**)

*Arts and Humanities Data Service (1998), Creating a Viable Scholarly Data Resource: an online Information Leaflet, found at **http://ahds.ac.uk/deposit/viable.html.**

*Buckland, M. (1999) The landscape of information science: The American Society For Information Science at 62, *Journal of the American Society of Information Science* Special Issue JASIS at 50, Wiley 1999. (This and other articles are found at the departmental Web site for the School of Information Management at the University of California, Berkeley **(http://www.sims.berkeley.edu/research/overview.html).**

Burnhill, P.(1985) *Towards the development of data libraries in the UK* Edinburgh: Centre for Application Software and Technology April 1985 (Prepared for the Committee of Librarians and Statisticians, a joint Library Association and the Royal Statistical Society body; and taken as evidence in the Joint Report by the ESRC/NSF Committee on Large-Scale Data Resources 1985)

Burnhill, P. and Tubby-Hille, M. E. (1994) On measuring the relation between social science research activity and research publication, Research Evaluation 4 (3), December.

Dempsey, L. (1998) Afterword: places and spaces, in *Towards the Digital Library:* The Initiatives for Access Programme, Carpenter, L., Shaw, S. and Prescott, A (eds;) The British Library London .

Hamilton, G. (1982) Access to statistics: a survey and a call for action, *Proceedings of 30th Annual Study Group, Oxford. Library Association Reference,* Special and Information Section, Library Association.

Kenny, A. (1998) Foreword to *Towards the Digital Library*: The Initiatives for Access Programme, The British Library, London.

Kirk, J (1982)Clement Little's Edinburgh, in *Edinburgh University Library*, 1580-1980: *a Collection of Historical Essays,* Guild, J. R. and A.(eds.) Edinburgh University Library Edinburgh.

Seeking Funding and Preparing Proposals

Ian Carter
Research and Enterprise
University of Glasgow

Introduction

The task of raising funds is all pervasive, whether for research projects or infrastructure. For researchers, it is required as a core skill from early in their career, whether to get funding for their postgraduate studies, or to fund their postdoctoral research. There is a large number of bodies who fund research in the United Kingdom, from all over the world (Glasgow University received awards from 480 different sponsors from 22 different countries in 1998/99) and the size of university-based research funding is large (£1,733M for project funding in 97/98), so one might think that there are plenty of opportunities. However, the funders tend to specialize in particular areas of interest, and there are many academic staff looking for funding (89,500 in 1997/98, which means only £19k per person - less than the cost of a researcher at the lowest point on the salary scale). There is thus a significant competition for funding.

The nature and process of applying for funding has changed over the past few years. Today, the average project proposal has to be more comprehensive and better justified, hitting specific areas of interest or targets set by the sponsor, and often involving partnerships, whether with people from other disciplines or with end users of the research.

When writing a proposal, one needs to make sure the 'science' is correct, high quality, well explained, and so on, but also to demonstrate best value, best fit with objectives, timing, and flexibility of approach. It is only the combination of these which will give the proposal the competitive edge it needs.

The political environment also needs to be fully considered. For example, over the last few years the Foresight process and related documentation have played a significant role in Government policy, and hence has to be addressed in relevant applications. Similarly, commercialization of research is a current topic. A good example of a scheme where a standard scientific proposal is not adequate is the Scottish Higher Education Funding Council's (SHEFC) Research Development Grant (RDG), where the benefits to research capability and the health and wealth of the nation have to be very clearly demonstrated. Indeed, an RDG proposal almost has to be written with an opposite balance to a standard proposal to a Research Council.

In most institutions, whether universities or not, a potential research subject or resource holding needs to fit into a strategic profile. The institutional strategy needs to be in tune with local, regional and national strategies, in order to maximise opportunities. In some cases this will mean full integration, in others it will involve complementarity so that alternatives are still possible.

The process of gaining funding is discussed more fully in the next section, but before doing so we should illustrate what we mean by 'resource' projects. A 'normal' research project tends to be about investigating an issue or a hypothesis, and reporting on the outcome or describing the discovery. A resource project is one whose purpose is to find, collate and present information or facilities which can then be used by researchers within other, specific projects. In other words, a resource project does not necessarily 'do' research as its primary aim, but enables others to undertake research through access to resources (in the broadest sense).

The difficulty the proposer of a resource project thus faces is in showing the benefits to be gained from creating the new resource. They need to be able to show the research that would be thus enabled, and to have suitable indications of users' enthusiasm for it.

Examples of resource projects include:

- special collections;
- unique, often expensive, equipment;
- records (data or written material);
- electronic archives (images, sound, video as well as text).

The Application Process

The process of applying for funding varies between sponsors, and whether the approach is speculative (e.g., the Research Councils' responsive mode), against a specification (e.g., a call for tenders), or in response to an enquiry. In some cases there will be a well-defined process, sometimes requiring both outline and full applications. In others there will be little or no guidance: many people find it harder to write a proposal given a blank sheet of paper than if they are very constrained by a detailed application form, despite the usual protests about the latter. Similarly, the acceptance may be a 'take it or leave it' offer from the funder, using their standard terms, or be a matter for commercial negotiation.

Whatever the process involved, several issues are always relevant. Having a good idea is only the first part of making a funding application!

Preparation

- Do your homework on the relevant funding bodies. Understand and target their interests. Find out what they have funded recently, in terms of both area and size. Be selective in choosing the best funding body for the idea. Undertaking a scattergun approach with a standard application will have as much chance of success as a similar approach to job applications.

- Discussing an idea for an application with the staff at the funding body can be very beneficial, as it can help to tune the application to the interests of the sponsor. Similarly, it can prevent a time-wasting application.

- Maintaining contact with a sponsor can help you to find out about special initiatives and policy changes, thereby being in a good position to respond. It can also help to give a funding body ideas for future initiatives.

- Do not confine yourself to a single sponsor, or to the 'usual' sources. In order to fund a project it may be necessary to attract funds from a number of different sponsors. However, when doing this it is vital to remember that each sponsor will have its own interests, terms and culture. This is particularly the case when mixing funding from public and private sectors. Government schemes which require co-funding from private industry can be the most complex to put together and manage.

- For grant applications, follow the funding bodies' rules, in terms of deadlines, length and structure of proposal, budget details and so on. This may sound obvious, but it is surprising how many people do not fill in the forms correctly - some bodies will automatically reject such applications.

- Discuss the application with others; get information and advice. A discussion with colleagues can help to refine and clarify the ideas and their presentation, and might also identify relevant sponsor-specific issues.

- Be very clear about ownership issues. Intellectual Property (IP) and copyright are complex areas, and it is dangerous to make assumptions about rights over objects, data and results. IP law differs between countries, so that particular care is needed for a project crossing national boundaries.

- Collaborative proposals take more time and effort to put together and to run, but they can open the door to funding. Some schemes require collaboration: some problems can only be solved through collaboration; for a newcomer to fund raising, collaboration can provide the first foot on the ladder. But be prepared to work hard at making the collaboration work, as there may be cultural, disciplinary or national differences within the team.

The Proposal

- Provide a good, strong, clear case, in English not technical jargon. Include a summary suitable for the intelligent lay person. The first two sentences of any proposal are the most important. The purpose of the proposal is to sell the idea, not to bamboozle the reader with the proposer's esoteric brilliance.

- Be specific in what, why, when, and how. Also be realistic, as both over and under ambitious projects will be found out.

- Do not use ninety per cent of the allowed length of proposal in presenting the background. A well written proposal contains a beginning, a middle and an end which relate to each other. This sounds like the ultimate in common sense, but many proposals do not achieve it.

- Present the track record of the proposer(s), to demonstrate that the funder can have confidence in their ability to deliver the project successfully, in terms of both subject expertise and project management capability. When entering a new field (or creating a new topic), demonstration of track record is just as relevant, as it will show that the proposer has done this sort of thing before, even if not in this precise area.

- Identify and fully justify all necessary costs to do the work. If the particular funder will not provide sufficient funding (e.g., because of a budget limit or because of inadmissible items, such as equipment or indirect costs), you will still need to fund these costs in order to do the work. This has always been important, but is increasingly so in the context of the Transparency Review of university costs (JCPSG, 1999).

- Leave enough time: it always takes longer than applicants think to prepare a proposal and get all the necessary authorisations. This is especially so for collaborative proposals. Also leave enough time before you want to start the work: most proposals take at least six months before they are awarded, and commercial negotiation can take several months.

The Award

- There is often confusion in academic circles about the differences between a grant and a contract. A grant *is* a form of contract, and there are legal and financial implications of not performing under a grant as there are under a contract. Most grants provide little or no liability cover from the sponsor.

- Most organizations will allow only certain individuals formally to accept an award or sign a contract. Unauthorised individuals signing agreements can cause difficulties for the organization and personal liability for the individual.

- Keep in contact with the funder, both as formally required through regular reports, but also on an informal basis. This not only helps to keep the funder in touch with what is going on, they may be able to help if problems arise. Waiting until an issue becomes serious before informing the funder will not improve your relationships, and might even lead to funding being withdrawn!

- Manage the project within the budget. Funders may consider an extension in time and / or funding level, but not if they are made frequently, or if it looks as if the need for an extension has arisen through lack of project management.

- Look for opportunities to promote the project throughout its lifetime, rather than just thinking about it at the end of the three-year term. This might take the form of early publications (although always be aware of intellectual property issues), or through publicity events. A public sector or charitable funder will almost always be interested in this happening.

These issues are covered in more depth, including practical advice from experienced proposers, in one of a series of four booklets funded by SHEFC, which is available via the Web (Wilson, 1999).

Resource Projects

The context of this symposium and this set of papers is one of creating scholarly resources. This paper's interpretation of a resource project is the creation of a set of information or a technical facility which enables scholarly and research activity to take place. The other papers in this collection report on some initiatives to achieve this and on specific projects. One of the key issues, from funding and management perspectives, is the distinction between activity to produce a resource, and activity in using that resource to undertake research. This distinction can often be blurred, which may lead to problems in delivering the full range and extent of the benefits which could be achieved.

One of the dangers can be that the proposer of a resource project really wants the resource only for their own research, rather than being able to show a wider requirement. Equally, the proposer may concentrate on doing their research, rather than managing the facility. A potential funder will want to be able to see the benefits arising, and how they match their own objectives, just as with other projects.

There are a few organizations, such as the Scottish Cultural Resources Access Network (SCRAN), whose whole purpose is to establish a resource, and the Economic and Social Research Council (ESRC) which has in the past had a dedicated Resource Centre scheme, but most resource projects are funded by organizations which perceive the resource as a means to an end rather than the end in itself. It is vital to remember this when developing a project proposal, as the target can be too easily missed. This distinction is equally important for the funder to remember, when specifying the call for proposals or tenders and when assessing the proposals.

The earlier list of example resource projects in the Introduction included electronic archives, which is a particularly interesting category. In the past, in order to study certain artefacts or material, one would have to travel to where they are stored. Digital imaging means that scarce or unique items can be made available to a wide audience much more easily. The challenge here is in the process of capturing the images and making them available, or more precisely in the context of this paper, how to get it funded. Although such a project might use state of the art techniques, and do so in an innovative way, these often do not have to be further developed, and hence it cannot be considered as 'research' in that field (i.e., in information capture). The benefits of capturing images will include the potential for scholarly study and for education, but also for wider 'public' access.

Libraries are, of course, the classic resource project, and we are seeing more combined electronic holdings, where one library or museum has the real thing, and a network of others can access the digital or holographic image. The Research Libraries Support Programme run by the combined Higher Education Funding Councils is a current example of an initiative to support the collection/ collation and virtual distribution of the combined information, possibly using advanced capture techniques.

However, the issue is broader than just the research libraries of the British universities and associated institutions: it extends into other public and private organisations. This then creates the challenge for funding, as there are several stakeholders and interested parties who together might be able to provide sufficient funding, but who individually may be interested in one specific aspect (e.g., one body might want only to fund research whereas another would want only to fund public access). For proposer(s) of a project which fits into this model, the task is to create and present a coherent case meeting all aspirations without the project becoming 'all things to all people', and hence not meeting any targets. The onus is also on the funders to be flexible enough in what they will fund and how they will fund it (administering a project funded from several sources each with its own ways of doing things can be a nightmare!).

Reverting to the funding issue, a sponsor might agree to help establish the facility, but is likely to expect it to be self-supporting in the longer term. This makes the facility a service centre, charging for usage, and requiring a proper business plan. Experience has shown that the academic community is not always good at planning or running such a business, and universities are rarely able to show the true costs of such facilities (although the current Transparency Review (JCPSG, 1999) should help to address this). Given the original desire for the facility, the business plan might include different granularities of access, from public to academic to commercial, with corresponding access charges.

A recent report (SURPC, 1999) commissioned by SHEFC and the Committee of Scottish Higher Education Principals (COSHEP) investigated the level of collaborative use of research facilities, along with the barriers and drivers to the creation and use of such facilities. The issues were grouped into People, Process, Institutional and Funding, reflecting the major areas which need to be addressed in delivering successful collaborative use. Resource projects are typically collaborative, either in their development and management, or in the range of customers they serve.

Running a resource centre or facility is not the same, per se, as running a research project. The development and management of a resource or facility is itself a complex task, requiring a set of competencies, which do not necessarily have to reside in one person (SURPC, 1999):

- scientific (to understand the use and prioritize requests for access);
- technical (to support the users and maintain the facility);
- people management (to deal with staff and customers);
- marketing (to attract customers);
- administrative (to run the access mechanism and provide user support);
- financial (to keep the books and to ensure financial sustainability);
- planning (to develop the facility and ensure sustainability).

Explaining the implications of this to a researcher who has a good idea for a new collection can help to clarify both the project itself, but also the role that that researcher might or might not play. If such an idea comes to fruition and is successful, with the original researcher remaining responsible for its operation, their amount of research time is likely to diminish quite severely, which may not be what they actually want. On the other hand, ceding control of the resource to someone else can sometimes be difficult for the individual.

The challenges for resource projects, then, are similar to other research projects in terms of defining what is planned and why, and in meeting sponsor needs, but are further complicated by the need to meet users' requirements and in the management required.

Future Directions for Funding

Over the last few years we have seen a number of changes in the way research funding is provided. The existence of the National Lottery has provided funding where none existed for some areas. Similarly, the creation of the Arts and Humanities Research Board, initiated in England, and joined by Scotland, provides an avenue for project funding which did not previously exist for these subjects. At the same time, Government sources, of all kinds, have encouraged the interaction with the users of research, be they industry and commerce, or policy makers and the public. It is important to note that 'users of research' do not have to be industrial, as it is recognised that research results can be used by other researchers as well as informing policy makers and raising public awareness of scientific and cultural issues.

The trends we are seeing in funding are that, whilst there is still a wide mix of sources and requirements, there is more evidence of collaboration, multidisciplinary and multinational, and more focused research demands. The following bullet points summarise the trends.

- More directed programmes and special initiatives. Some of the Research Councils went through a phase of increasing the amount of research funded under directed programmes, where the area of work was quite tightly defined, and related to industrial needs. Although these have reduced slightly, there are more special initiatives, targeted at encouraging research in specific areas. For the Research Councils, following the last Comprehensive Spending Review, this typically involves areas related to genomics.

- There will be more multi- and interdisciplinary research. The special initiatives previously mentioned tend to be of this form, and multiple disciplines tend to be needed to solve complex user-based problems. This will also mean that there will be fewer applications from indiividuals.

- This in turn means that there will be more collaborative research, which takes more effort and management to deliver successfully. Multidisciplinary research can also challenge the internal management arrangements of universities, and the reporting and assessment processes of the higher education sector when a project is multi-institutional.

- There will be more user-oriented research, whether it is industry sponsored or led, or where it is delivering policy advice. There will also be a larger amount of industrial collaboration, as a means of tapping more research funds, in particular in areas where the public sector funding is not growing. This raises challenges in the form and style of delivery of research results, as they need to be oriented towards the user, and delivered on time.

- Researchers and universities will have to show more evidence of active dissemination, exploitation and use of their research skills and results. This will include non-research interactions with other organizations, which challenges the current performance metrics in the sector.

In this scenario, more time will be spent in creating and managing a project. We will have to become more proficient and efficient at the various elements of project management, especially where it involves multiple partners. We will also be involved in activities which span disciplines and which span the broad areas of research, education and 'community interaction' whilst delivering against harder (i.e., more defined) objectives.

Conclusions

The need to raise funds for activities, and to justify their use is a pervasive factor. Therefore, the skills needed to do so, and to manage the projects funded, are a vital part of a researcher's armoury. The ability to develop, present and defend a case pays dividends not only in funding terms, but also in using the same skills to present political arguments about the broader funding issues.

The creation of facilities and resources which underpin research and educational activity needs to be addressed by researchers, their institutions and the potential funders within a context which recognizes that they are different from standard research projects, and require elements of collaboration and service delivery.

References

Web Sites

JCPSG, 1999   Transparency Review of Research. Joint Costing and Pricing Steering Group. 1999. (**http://www.bris.ac.uk/JCPSG/transpar/index.htm**)

SURPC, 1999   Collaboration in the Use of Research Facilities. Scottish Universities Research Policy Consortium. 1999.

http://www.stir.ac.uk/research/surpc/collab.html

Wilson, W. K. 1999   Gaining Funding for Research. Universities of Edinburgh, Glasgow and Strathclyde. 1999. (http://www.gla.ac.uk/RandE/research-training/)

The Electronic Edition of the Correspondence of James McNeill Whistler

Nigel Thorp and Graeme Cannon
Centre for Whistler Studies
University of Glasgow

James McNeill Whistler, the American-born painter and etcher (1834-1903), was one of the most influential artists in Britain in the second half of the nineteenth century. He was acknowledged as a master of etching at an early age, and his controversial position as a painter, as well as his own publications, kept him in the forefront of public attention throughout his career. In 1878 he brought a celebrated lawsuit for libel against the critic John Ruskin in order to defend the artist's right to challenge adverse criticism. Although he worked principally in England and France, he was awarded many international honours, and he had followers throughout Europe and North America. In a career of over fifty years, he produced some 3000 works of art, almost 1000 of which are in the University of Glasgow, which owns Whistler's literary and artistic estate.

The University material includes the largest single collection of his correspondence and papers, his library, and furniture and other possessions. Glasgow scholars have been responsible for the catalogue raisonné of Whistler's oil paintings (Young et al., 1980) and of his drawings, pastels and watercolours (MacDonald, 1995). The University has organized or contributed to numbers of exhibitions over the years, most notably the international Whistler exhibition at the Tate Gallery, the Musée d'Orsay and the National Gallery of Art in Washington in 1994-95. In 1992 the University established the Centre for Whistler Studies, with the edition of the Whistler correspondence as its major research project.

The Whistler Correspondence
The Whistler correspondence, of some 10,000 letters, constitutes a

highly important source of information, not only for the artist himself, but also for the study of European and American art in the second half of the nineteenth century. The letters record his contacts with fellow artists, dealers, collectors, literary figures, and a wide circle of acquaintance in the United Kingdom (UK), France and the United States. In addition to documenting the development of his own art, they throw light on many of the central issues of art and art criticism of the day, including the Aesthetic movement in the UK and the development of Symbolism. No other artist of the period has left such an extensive record of his career. Although some 750 of his letters have been published over the past 100 years, this is less than one twelfth of the edition which is now in progress.

The edition of the Whistler correspondence was planned over twenty years ago, but it only emerged as a practical possibility in the early 1990s, with the development of electronic text-editing systems and the support of a succession of grants from the British Academy. This has continued with the current Institutional Fellowships from the Humanities Research Board (now the Arts and Humanities Research Board) for two full-time Research Fellows, Dr Margaret MacDonald and Dr Patricia de Montfort, as editors, for 1996-2003: these fellowships will see the edition through to 2003, the centenary of Whistler's death.

During the first stage of the project, 1991-95, a survey of over 2,000 public and private collections world-wide was conducted to locate Whistler correspondence not previously recorded in Glasgow. Details of some 12,000 letters were entered into a database and copies of the letters were made for preliminary editorial work, including dating. The edition is expected to include a total of around 10,000 letters: all 5,500 letters written by Whistler between the beginning of his artistic career in 1855 and his death in 1903, some 3,000 letters written to him, and 1,500 letters written on his behalf or closely connected with him.

The Centre has formal research links with the Freer Gallery of Art, Smithsonian Institution, Washington, which houses the largest collection of Whistler's work in North America, and with the Delaware Art Museum. The organization of the project includes the opportunity for contributions from other Whistler scholars, who provide supplementary annotations in particular subject areas. These include Dr Linda Merrill, formerly at the Freer Gallery, who has published extensively on Whistler in the 1860s and 1870s, and Dr Joy Newton, at the University of Glasgow, who has concentrated on Whistler's contacts with.French literary figures: the Centre also has contacts with other specialists in nineteenth-century art in Washington, Chicago, Toronto, Paris, Amsterdam and elsewhere.

Electronic Structures

The whole of the Whistler correspondence is being edited in electronic form, for publication in CD-Rom or other appropriate format. The system allows scanned images of letters, works of art and other reference material such as photographs and maps to be included in the edition and allows edited letters to be viewed on a Web browser. It is intended to make a wide selection of letters available for consultation on the Web, and to publish a selection of 1200-1500 letters in book form when the electronic edition is complete.

The size of the undertaking, and the time limit on the core funding, means that the project is very much concerned with through-put, and we have needed to approach the questions of process as well as of scholarship in the light of what a small team of scholars without great IT expertise can manage to achieve within the time limit. We have consulted the Arts and Humanities Data Service (AHDS) on a regular basis, particularly for advice from the Oxford Text Archive (OTA) on electronic editing systems. We have also benefited extensively from discussions with Michael Pidd at the Humanities Research Institution in Sheffield and with a number of scholars at the University of Virginia's Institute for Advanced Technology in the Humanities.

A trial format for a multimedia edition was made in 1997 using Hyper Text Markup Language (HTML). An assessment of the strengths of the HTML approach emphasized the availability of user-friendly reliable editing programs (e.g., SoftQuad's HotMetal), which allowed the editorial team to become proficient relatively rapidly. The weaknesses included the temptation to commit resources to creating large numbers of links between files, the non-specific mark-up, and matters relating to the style of presentation being included in the document rather than in the overall control structure. The HTML system was adopted as a temporary solution for annotating transcriptions while the development of the Standard Genralised Markup Language (SGML) system was in progress.

A number of issues needed to be considered on gathering the information and choosing portable file formats, the chief one of them being the unsuitability of proprietary word-processor file formats and the limitations of pure ASCII text (American Standard Code for International Interchange). Factors preventing the early adoption of SGML included the cost of publishing software, the need for a user-friendly SGML editing system, and the delays involved in working with an initial system, the results of which could not be accurately predicted.

The availability of SoftQuad's SGML Publishing Suite for Research Collections at a reduced price allowed evaluation of the product in relation to the needs of the project. The development of electronic systems to combine database reference tables and annotated texts of letters marked-up in SGML was largely completed in 1997/98. Letters are now marked up in SGML, using SoftQuad's Author/Editor program, with a DTD (Document Type Definition, or system of rules) designed for the project. The system adopted allows individual files to be linked to the core database and also for the same files to be included in larger SGML groupings of the correspondence. The use of driver files for single documents as well as larger groupings puts limitations, however, on the use of internal and external links. DTDs for biographies, works of art and geographical locations are currently being added to the reference resources.

Notes are linked to the text and appear in a separate box or at the foot of the letter, depending on the viewing style selected; the project uses an additional style approximating to a conventional printed page format when providing texts in printed form for consultation, and the SGML mark-up allows readers also to set their own viewing preferences if they wish.

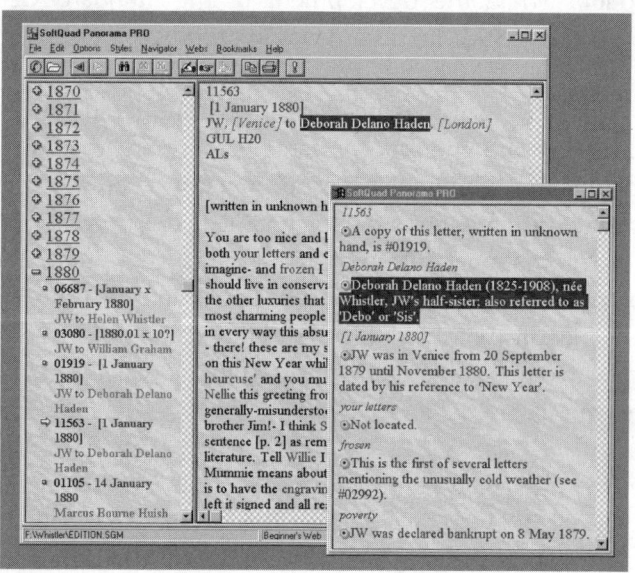

The complete edition of Whistler correspondence with navigation frame (left hand side) and a note in a separate window activated by a hyperlink in the text.

The notes incorporate links to text entities which insert standard descriptions in all instances in which each entity is used. The text entities, which ensure uniformity of description and permit global updating of reference data, are currently used for biographical and bibliographical descriptions.

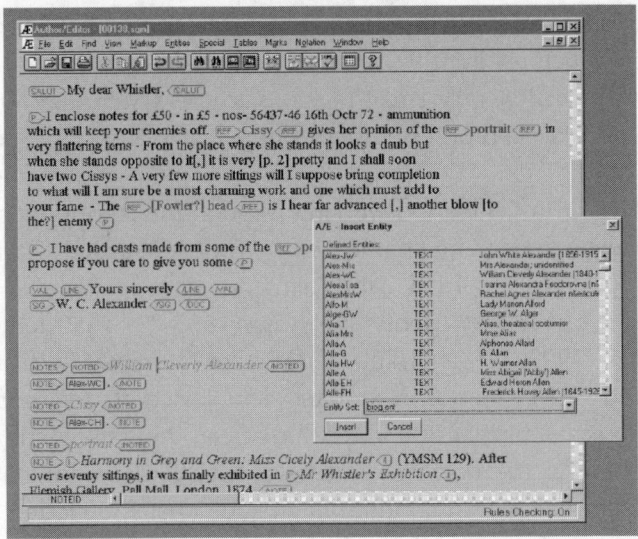

Editing a transcription in Author/Editor, showing how a text entity from a separate file can be inserted from a drop-down menu.

Although the editors came to the project with IT skills limited to a knowledge of word-processing and not much else, we have settled fairly easily into the procedures required by SGML and the relational database system. We have also found that the project assistants whom we have been able to take on this year have quickly learned how to transcribe letters straight into the marked-up format: this is the preferred way of working, as it takes almost as long to transfer a previously keyboarded letter into the SGML format as it does to make a marked-up transcription from scratch. Instructions for transcriptions, data entry and mark-up, and guidelines and standards for editorial method, are set out in an editorial handbook, which is updated with any revisions required.

The rate at which letters that can be annotated and indexed depends of course on the length and complexity of the letters. It is also influenced by the volume of new information that needs to be added to the reference databases, and by the requirements of other areas of research and development for the project, including research visits to archives. The development of the mark-up system and reference structures in 1997/98 occupied a considerable amount of time, but now that only small revisions to the system are required, the rate of editorial progress is increasing.

The editorial team is working through the correspondence in chronological order, beginning with Whistler's arrival as an art student in Paris in 1855, and aims to have completed initial annotation of the first twenty-five years (1855-79, 1650 letters) by December 1999. Over 1,200 letters are currently available in completed SGML format, annotated and linked to reference and index sources. A further 800 letters have been transcribed and linked by hyperlink to the database but have not yet been annotated or indexed. Unverified transcriptions of an additional 1300 letters which were available from a variety of sources have also been converted into SGML format. This leaves some 6,750 letters to be transcribed into SGML – approximately 2,250 letters per year for three years, or eleven letters per day.

The letters database is supported by relational tables and other databases currently including 3000 personal names, 500 institutional names, 3000 works of art, 250 exhibitions, a bibliography of 1700 titles, and a chronology with 4000 entries. From an original flat-file database structure in 1991 listing letters from all sources, the project migrated to MicroSoft Access when consolidating various databases in 1996. The flat-file structure was expanded to a relational structure in order to reduce the duplication of information and facilitate global changes and updating.

Letters are indexed for personal names, institutions, works of art, exhibitions, places, and other versions of the letter text as part of the annotation procedure. Full-text searching is available for all letters as they are added to the electronic edition; subject indexing is carried out for each period of the correspondence as it is completed.

Letter texts and annotations prepared by one editor are routinely checked by a second editor. They are then reviewed for content and style by all three editors on a cumulative basis for each period as it is completed to ensure consistency of approach. Copy-editing is carried out for each year of the correspondence when editorial work is complete. An editorial board of scholars in the United Kingdom and the United States advises on general editorial matters: sample groups of letters are sent periodically to the members of the Board, who include a nominee of the British Academy, and their responses are circulated and discussed.

Editorial Work

Each of the full-time editors specialises in particular material: Dr MacDonald on works of art and dealers, Dr de Montfort on literature and criticism, and Dr Thorp on Whistler's life in France and his French contacts.

The editors' task is to ensure the accuracy of the edited texts, to provide a full explanation of both the content and the context of the correspondence, and to achieve the most manageable and efficient means of providing access to the texts and editorial information. Although the editorial work must concentrate on the textual content and chronology for the project to be completed within the expected time-scale, plans allow for the inclusion of reference images of works of art when these can be made available.

The editors carry out the main process of research and annotation, broadly in step with the provision of preliminary texts by the project assistants. The need for half of the correspondence to be dated more precisely in order to fit within the chronological sequence makes substantial demands on editorial time, but the increased provision of transcriptions made by project assistants is making this initial task considerably more expeditious.

Although initial transcriptions are made from photocopies of the originals, or print-out from microfilm, all edited texts will be checked by the editors against the originals as part of standard editorial procedures. Over sixty per cent of the original correspondence is in Glasgow, but substantial periods of time need to be spent in other collections, chiefly in Washington (2400 letters), but also in New York (300 letters), and London (250 letters).

The editors will follow up contacts and clues in other places to find related material and answer specific research queries. Unrecorded letters still emerge, including a recent group of documents which throw further light on the circumstances of Whistler's six-month stay in Valparaiso in 1866: this episode in his life has always puzzled his biographers and appears to be linked more closely than he admitted to championing the cause of Chilean resistance to Spanish forces then blockading sea lanes in the southern Pacific! Additional archival research is needed to follow up such leads disclosed during editorial work, but the total number of letters is not expected to increase significantly.

The editors also write explanatory essays on significant issues, including general surveys of each year and of important periods (such as Whistler and his contemporaries in Venice, 1879-80), subjects (such as *Japonisme)*, and institutions (such as the International Society of Sculptors, Painters and Gravers).

Each editor will write biographies of people, such as family members, collectors and dealers, who are not covered, or not adequately covered, by the principal published biographies: some 300 of these are estimated to be needed. The editors will seek to establish the identity of all other people mentioned and write brief biographies of them for the biographical database.

After 2003, the electronic edition will be updated with any further Whistler letters that come to light for the period 1855-1903. There are plans also to supplement the correspondence for the years of Whistler's career with family and professional letters relating to Whistler dating from before 1855 and after his death.

Project Funding

The edition has been supported by annual grants from the British Academy for a research assistant, 1991-96, and by two British Academy Humanities Research Board Institutional Fellowships, 1996-2003. The project is now one of the core research projects funded by the British Academy Committee on Academy Research Projects, which has made further grants in support of computing advice, clerical support and travel costs of contributing editors. Other awards and grants have been made by the Sloan Foundation, the Delaware Art Museum, the University of Glasgow Faculty of Arts, and private donors. The overall costs of a large-scale project of this kind are indicated by the fact that the total value of these awards to date, covering the period 1991-2000, is some £400,000. The University of Glasgow provides the salary of the Director of the Whistler Centre and, until the current year, all overhead costs.

Copyright

Although the University of Glasgow owns Whistler's copyright, there is the need to identify current copyright ownership of letters written by people other than Whistler himself and to obtain permission for their letters to be published. Legal opinion obtained by the University suggests that, if works are more than 100 years old and have been in a public collection for more than 50 years, the Copyright Act 1988 provides a defence against an action for breach of copyright in the U.K. where an attempt has been made to trace a copyright holder but the attempt has been unsuccessful.

References

MacDonald, M. F.(1995), *James McNeill Whistler. Drawings, Pastels and Watercolours. A Catalogue Raisonné*, New Haven and London.

Young,, A. M., MacDonald, M. F., Miles, H. and Spencer, R.(1980): *The Paintings of James McNeill Whistler*, New Haven and London.

Photographic Archives: Aberdeen, Dundee and St Andrews

Norman H. Reid
University Library
St Andrews University

When William Henry Fox Talbot announced his invention of a negative-positive photographic process to a meeting of the Royal Society in London in January 1839, it was a moment which was to have a profound effect on modern life. For it was this process, rather than others introduced by, for example, the Frenchman Louis Daguerre, which was to become the forerunner of modern photography, the art, science and common, everyday tool we now take so much for granted. St Andrews - better known for its connections with the history of the church in Scotland, or for a certain sporting involvement - is inextricably linked with the history of photography. Largely consequent upon Fox Talbot's longstanding acquaintance with Sir David Brewster, then Principal of the United College of St Andrews University, Talbot's invention became the subject of a great deal of interested experimentation in St Andrews, and it, along with the other experimental photographic processes of the period, were frequently the focus of display and discussion in the meetings of the newly-founded Literary and Philosophical Society of St Andrews (The Society's Minute Books survive within the muniment collections of St Andrews University -SAUL UY8525).

Photographic Collections at St Andrews, Aberdeen and Dundee

It comes as no surprise, therefore, to learn that the great luminaries of early Scottish photography have St Andrews connections. Dr John Adamson, perhaps to be regarded as the 'father' of Scottish photography, was a local medical practitioner, part-time lecturer in the University, Secretary of the Literary and Philosophical Society, and friend of Brewster. The most famous of the early photographic partnerships, Hill and Adamson, was formed when John Adamson's younger brother Robert linked with the Edinburgh artist David Octavius Hill for an extraordinarily creative five-year period before Adamson's early death in 1848. Even the Provost of St Andrews, Sir Hugh Lyon Playfair, joined Brewster's group of enthusiasts. Brewster's influence, and the continuing interest of his successors (such as James David Forbes, his immediate successor, who was the first British scientist to visit Daguerre's studio in Paris in 1839, and who recorded his excitement in journals and correspondence - SAUL msdep 7/15/118, msdep 7/1839/29), ensured that the developing art was well represented in the University's library. Complete copies of both of Talbot's early published albums, Pencil of Nature (1844) and 'Sun Pictures in Scotland' (1845), were bought by the library on publication, and survive intact. Albums replete with the photographs of the early masters, and joined also by the works of slightly later practitioners such as Thomas Rodger (who set up one of the earliest commercial photographic studios in the country in St Andrews in 1849) - form what is today one of the world's leading research collections.

The library has, over the years, added to this core of early material large collections of the works of single photographers or photographic firms (most notably, perhaps, the negatives of Robert Moyes Adam (1885-1967), the renowned Scottish landscape photographer; and the surviving monochrome image archive of J. Valentine & Co., the Dundee-based firm which, after almost forty years in portrait and landscape photography, launched themselves into the picture postcard market towards the end of the nineteenth century, and became one of the world's largest postcard publishers.) The St Andrews collection, therefore, numbering over 300,000 images and still growing, forms one of the largest general photographic collections in Scotland with a wide-ranging geographical, subject and chronological coverage, which makes it truly a research resource of international standing.

The Universities of Aberdeen and Dundee, though not in a position to claim such an impressive photographic pedigree, are nonetheless no small players in the world of photography. Aberdeen is best known for being home to the George Washington Wilson collection (personal communication, D I. Beavan). Containing images dating from c.1859-1908, it forms the surviving image archive of a company which was formed in 1851/52. Similar in some respects to St Andrew's Valentine archive, in that the company's primary business was 'tourist photography', the collection is an unrivalled source for the study of the history and culture not just of the North and North East of Scotland in the Victorian and Edwardian periods, but also of Scotland as a whole, Great Britain and overseas. Relatively few of Valentine's foreign images are known to have survived, but within the George Washington Wilson Collection there are images from colonial Australia, South Africa and the Mediterranean round Gibraltar. These have attracted considerable ethnographic as well as socio-historical interest. The 40,000 images which comprise this archive were acquired by the University Library in 1954. In addition, the collection has been the subject of a selective publication programme which has presented some seventy images with brief contextual history on themes such as Royal Deeside, the Hebrides, and Dundee and Angus. A conference was held in Aberdeen University in 1997 under the title 'By royal appointment; Aberdeen's pioneer photographer George Washington Wilson 1823-1893' (the papers of which are held in the Library) studied his life and work and the broader historical and cultural issues.

Dundee's primary collection is the archive of Michael Peto, a Hungarian photo-journalist who died in 1970 (Personal communication Mrs P Whatley). Peto's is an interesting history, for he came late to photography, following the war period, which he spent working for the Ministry of Labour, acting as personal secretary to Count Karolyi, helping to plan for the hoped-for post war 'New Democratic Hungary'. The early photographs therefore provide a record of lifestyle and social conditions in Eastern Europe, particularly

Budapest, in the immediate post-war period. They show a way of life which has changed beyond all recognition, and in some ways has ceased to exist. But the collection is not limited in either geographical or subject terms. With the eye of an artist and the concern of a humanitarian, Peto travelled widely throughout Europe, the Middle and Far East and India, working for much of his career on a freelance basis for The Observer and for Save the Children Fund. His photographs feature many personalities in politics and the arts during the 1950s and 1960s (including rare photographs of C.S. Lewis) and a fine coverage of the London ballet 'rehearsal' scene in the period during which Rudolph Nureyev arrived. The complete collection, comprising some 128,000 prints, negatives and transparencies, was gifted by Peto's family to Dundee University in 1971. Much of the original order of the collection was destroyed during its transfer, and early work entailed re-organization and identification of the images. In 1976-77 a Job Creation Programme, assisted by financial aid from various other sources, allowed the film negatives to be cleaned and rehoused. Approximately ten per cent of the negatives were printed, identified, classified and bound into over 250 albums, but, although the collection has been regularly used within a variety of publications (e.g., Harris, 1988), a huge amount of work remains before its research potential can be fully explored.

Meeting the Increasing Demand for Photography

Photography is increasingly in demand by the academic community. Since early times, of course, the practice has been to accompany academic writings with pictures which emphasize or illustrate the thesis presented. As soon as photography became a viable tool for such illustration it began to be used in this way. Cheaper and better means of reproducing photographs in print, along with an inexorable drive to render academic work more popular, and hence more visually attractive, have led to an increasing use of illustrative photography. This, however, is not the reason for the enormous increase in demand for access to photography over the past few years. Rather, we are witnessing a changing attitude towards the photograph itself. In times past the urban historian, for example, would construct a thesis on the basis of documentary, architectural, cartological, archaeological and perhaps even oral evidence. The completed work might then be illustrated with photographs of varying types, used to bolster the ideas already formed. Now, there is a growing tendency to use the photograph as part of the primary evidence itself, obvious enough in the example just cited, or in the field of art history, but in other areas of study perhaps less so. Historians of the natural world, the environment, the built environment, social and economic change, warfare, politics, and many other subjects are using photography as primary evidence. The George Washington Wilson catalogues, for instance, like those of his rival, Valentine of Dundee, provide 'both a map and an index of the popularity of the tourist destinations of Scotland' (Smart, 1988) and have been used by economic historians to plot the links between tourism and commercial photography in Scotland as well as the development of sport and leisure in the context of tourism as an indigenous industry. (e.g., Durie, 1988) The coastal work of Robert Moyes Adam is currently being used to inform a Leverhume-funded research project on Scottish photoecology. (Crawford, in progress) A work regarding socio-environmental change has made significant use of photographic evidence (Smout and Lambert, forthcoming) These few examples serve to illustrate the trend towards the use of photography as primary source material, and present the photographic archivist with the task of meeting an increasing demand for access to the collections.

The archivist's task is daunting, because photographic collections are notoriously difficult to use. There are two primary problems. Firstly, a balance must be maintained between the conflicting requirements of access and preservation. Photographs are delicate: they are particularly susceptible to damage by light, and in many of their forms they are also physically fragile. They fade, crack, peel and display other symptoms of degradation which can render them at best useless, and at worst hazardous to the user. Negatives prior to the introduction of modern celluloid film will either be on glass or on paper, and are as susceptible to damage through over-use as any other flimsy archival artefact. There are within these collections thousands of images for which no prints exist, which are physically difficult to examine, even if they are in good condition. If a researcher is eventually successful in negotiating the hazards of consulting the collections, and identifies an image which requires to be copied, then a fragile original, perhaps a century old or more, has to be subjected to the handling and processing demands of the modern darkroom. Clearly, archivists are faced in these circumstances with an extreme example of the age-old discontinuity of their profession: the tension between the two conflicting duties of providing access and of preserving the archives.

There is, however, an additional complicating factor. Traditional archives, the primary evidential value of which is generally contained within the written word, are relatively easy to describe. To an extent, they can be indexed to provide at least a rudimentary guide to their content and utility without the researcher requiring to access them. The traditional archive descriptive list - or its modern database equivalent - is therefore the first search filter which the researcher uses in order to refine the search and identify the comparatively few archival items which will be of use. The provision of this intellectual access to photography represents an entirely different challenge. The archive list or index, in its traditional form, is entirely inadequate to provide access to an image archive. Personal and/or place name indices can be useful, but only for very limited purposes, and for very specific enquiries. Subject indices are perhaps more helpful, but are still limited in coverage and depth, and can be extremely large and cumbersome to use in the context of numerous and complex collections.

Such tools are helpful only for the limited use of photography as illustration. The less passive use of the image however – in its rôle as primary evidence – places far greater demands on the access tools. The index may identify a photograph of an event, and might even use cross-references to identify location and individuals present. It would be a sophisticated index indeed, however, that could offer any sort of search access based on the architectural or environmental context of the photograph, the weather conditions, the mode and state of dress of onlookers, the mood or expressions of the protagonists. The level of access required by the modern researcher demands that the collections are opened up to the possibilities of such research activity. Indeed, since financial restraints often render it necessary for such collections to be at least partially self-supporting, it becomes necessary to look to other, equally demanding, markets. The commercial user of historic photography frequently brings a further complication – the issue of urgency. The academic research project tends to be a long-term activity, and thus identifying and copying the right image is generally not a particularly urgent task. For the advertiser, the newspaper or magazine, however, a few hours' delay can be crucial. The ability to identify suitable images from an increasingly diverse range of criteria, and produce useable copies within a very short time scale becomes a prerequisite of any access system.

The Application of Digital Technology

The three Universities under discussion have all been aware of these difficulties for some time. In Aberdeen, readers and researchers have had to rely on a variety of search facilities within the University itself to appreciate the full extent of the George Washington Wilson collection. In Dundee, the provision of album prints was an attempt to make some of the collection visible to the enquirer, and in St Andrews a large and complex series of hard-copy indices has provided only a rudimentary, and slow, level of access. It has been clear to all three Universities for some years that digital technology offered perhaps the only solution to these dual problems. The powerful search facilities of a database containing descriptions of the photographs offer a level and speed of intellectual access which cannot be matched in any other way. Complemented by the availability of the images themselves in digital form, thus overcoming the difficulties of physical access outlined above, the database becomes a research tool quite unparalleled in any traditional form. The additional benefits of on-screen manipulation, enhancement and comparison of the images, and the ability to produce high-quality copies without recourse to the original media, make the image-base a resource which not only provides information of which the traditional researcher could only have dreamed, but which also reduces the wear and tear on the fragile artefacts. An equal benefit, of course, is the ability, using the Internet, to allow remote access to the collections. Researchers, now able to interrogate the collection from their desktops, can achieve a far greater level of access without using the staff resources of the archive, and copies of images, of publishable quality, can be provided virtually on demand.

Aberdeen was the first to recognize that digital technology had the potential to open the collection to much wider use. As part of the University's digitization programme funded by the Joint Higher Education Funding Councils' Non-Formula Funding of Research Collections in the Humanities initiative (NFF), selections of the overseas images were digitally captured and web-mounted with an accompanying search engine (accessed through the Aberdeen gateway site at http//www abdn. Ac.uk/diss/heritage/). St Andrews followed soon after, launching a pilot project run with the assistance of the British Library (which was at that time embarked upon its PIX project (see Carey, 1998)). This pilot, funded by the University with NFF assistance, achieved the digitization of the fifteen thousand glass negatives in the Robert Moyes Adam Collection. The library's overall photographic digitization programme then continued with support from various sources, most significantly eLib's Higher Education Library Image Exchange (HELIX) programme, which brought together St Andrews University, de Montfort University and the Hulton-Getty Picture Library in a project to provide a single-search gateway to a large body of images within the partner's individual image-bases (www.helix.dmu.ac.uk/). A succession of grants from other sources (such as, for instance, the Scottish Cultural Resources Access Network (SCRAN)) have been utilized to maintain the digitization programme, which has now achieved the provision of some 65,000 electronic images, and the detailed database indexing of over 30,000. Until recently the image-base was available only locally, but a recent development has been the provision of a web-site (http.//basenet.st-and.ac.uk/) carrying a limited number of images, which will be gradually increased, eventually to encompass the bulk of the collection. Dundee has not yet begun the digitization of the Peto collection, but it is an ambition which is about to come to fruition.

The recent allocation of funds by the Joint Higher Education Funding Councils under the Research Support Libraries Programme (RSLP)offered the three Universities the opportunity to come together in a collaborative project to extend the digitization programmes of Aberdeen and St Andrews, and to make a start to the provision of access to Dundee's resources. A grant of £300,000 has been made for a project named 'The Visual Evidence', which aims, during 2000-2001 to digitize almost 100,000 photographs, all of which will be available through the web-sites of the three partners. In addition, a single-search interface will be introduced, so that the three image-bases will act to the researcher as one, providing a 'one-stop-shop' for what will become in time easily the largest and most wide-ranging photographic archive freely available within the Higher Education sector.

At the beginning of its programme, St Andrews University chose to use a proprietary image presentation software produced by iBase Imaging Systems of Ilkley, which has also provided the web-site. The present RSLP project allows for the adoption of the same software by Aberdeen and Dundee, thus creating a mutually supportive cluster of users in Scottish Higher Education, making the implementation of the single-search facility much easier.

Between them, the three universities have collections which amount to almost half a million images, ranging in date from the earliest days of photography to the present day, and of immense variety and subject-range. The provision of this level of access to all of them will be a long-term task which we are well aware is fraught with many technical, professional and financial difficulties. The problems notwithstanding, we aim to create an outstanding world-wide photographic resource for researchers from many different disciplines, both within and outwith the academic community.

References

Carey, P. (1998) PIX Project, in Carpenter, L., Shaw,S. and Prestcott, A. (eds.) *Towards the Digital Library: The Initiatives for Access Programme.* British Library, London.

Crawford, R.M.M., Professor of Plant Ecology, University of St Andrews: 'A Study of the Photoecology of Scotland since 1840", work in progress.

Durie, A J (1988) *George Washington Wilson, Sport and Leisure in Victorian Scotland,* Lancaster.

Harris, K.(1967) *About Britain,* London.

Smart, R. N.(1988)'Famous Throughout the World': Valentine & Sons Ltd., Dundee, *Rwview of Scottish Culture,* 4, 75-87.

Smout, T.C. and Lambert, R. A.(forthcoming) (eds)., *Nature and People on a Highland Estate, 1500-2000* .

Photograph Acknowledgments
Plates reproduced with permission of St Andrews University Library and iBase Imaging Systems Ltd.

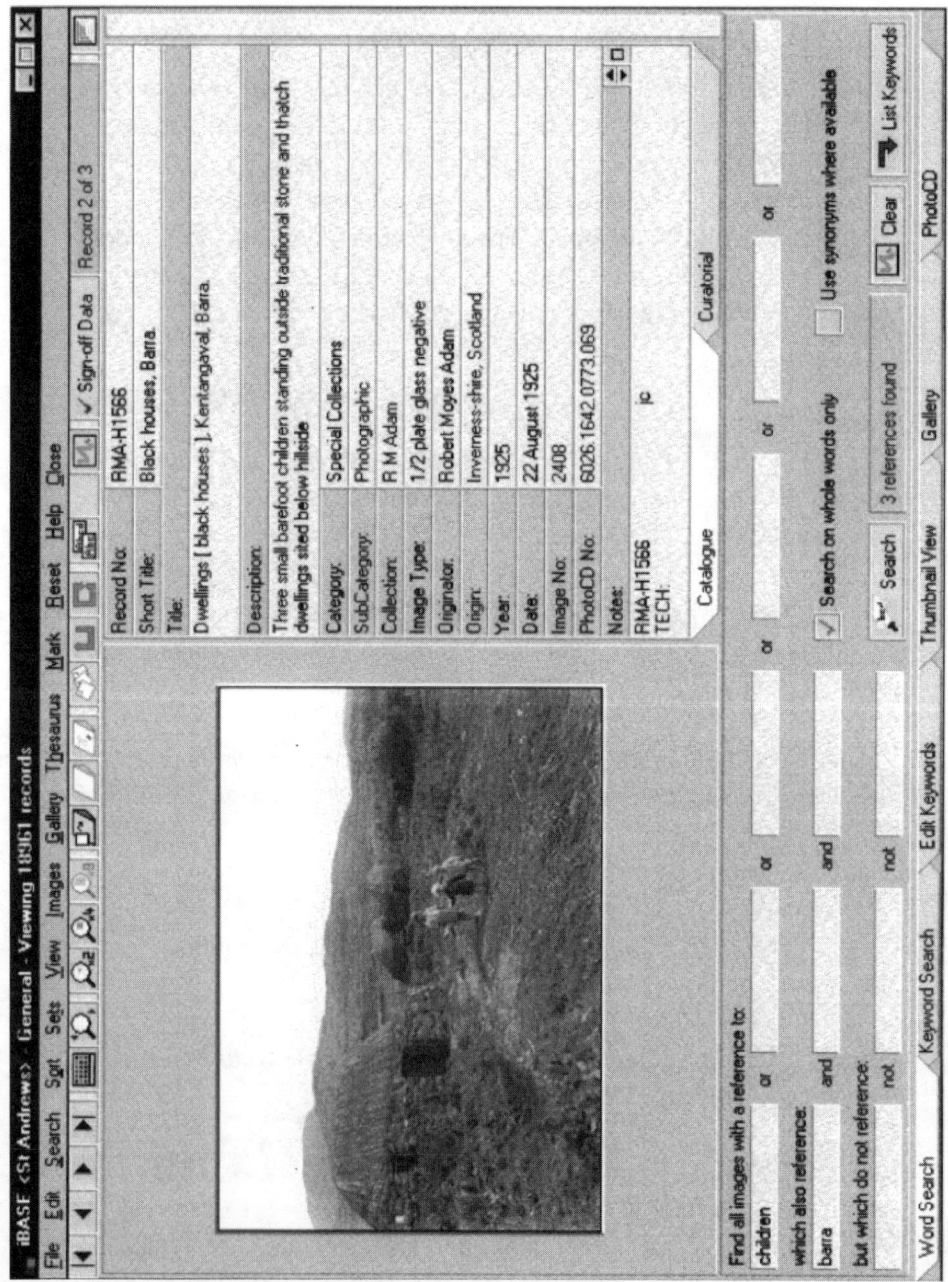

iBase: reference/data screen

iBase: image detail screen

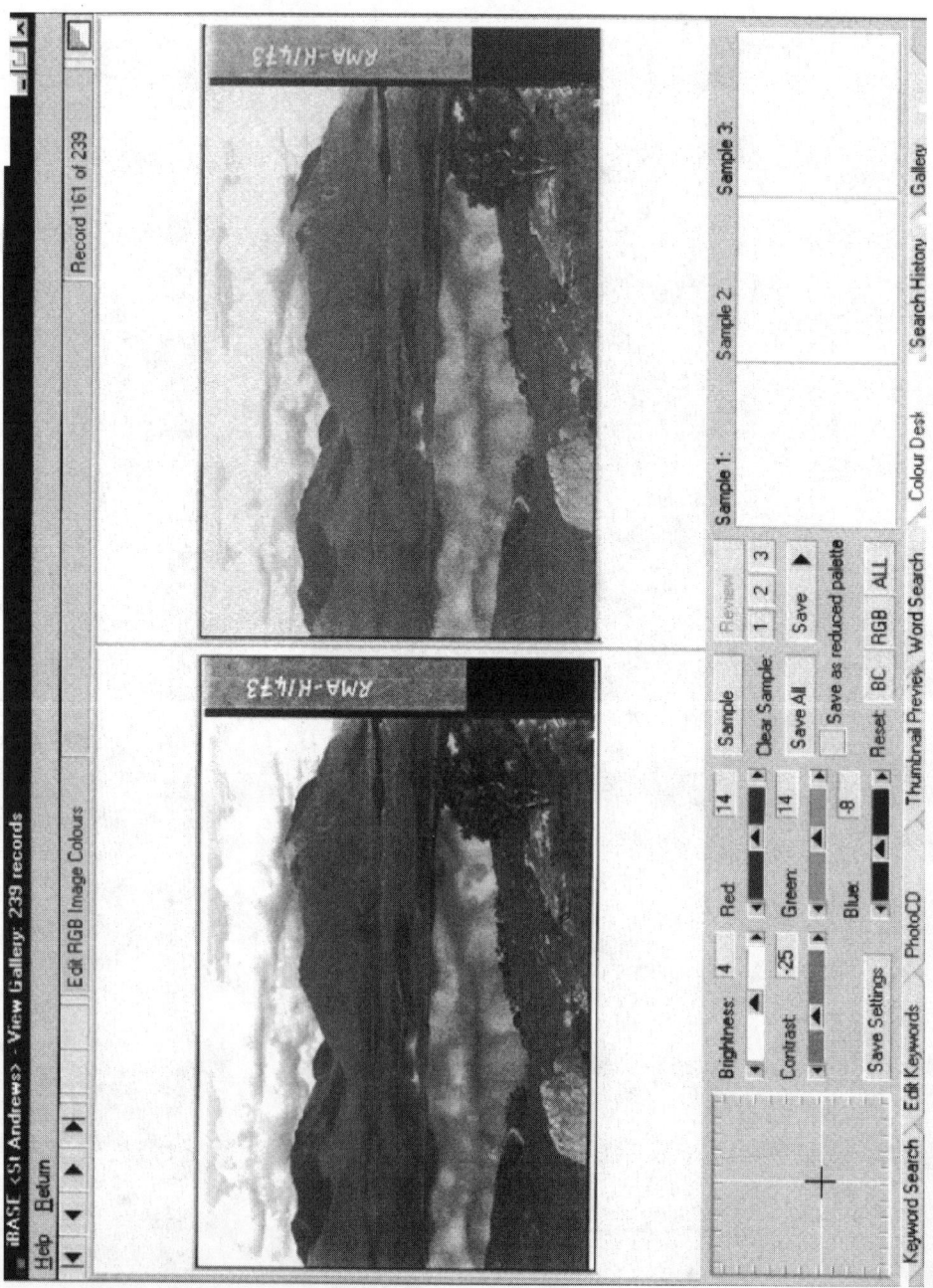

iBase: colour/intensity/contrast manipulation

118

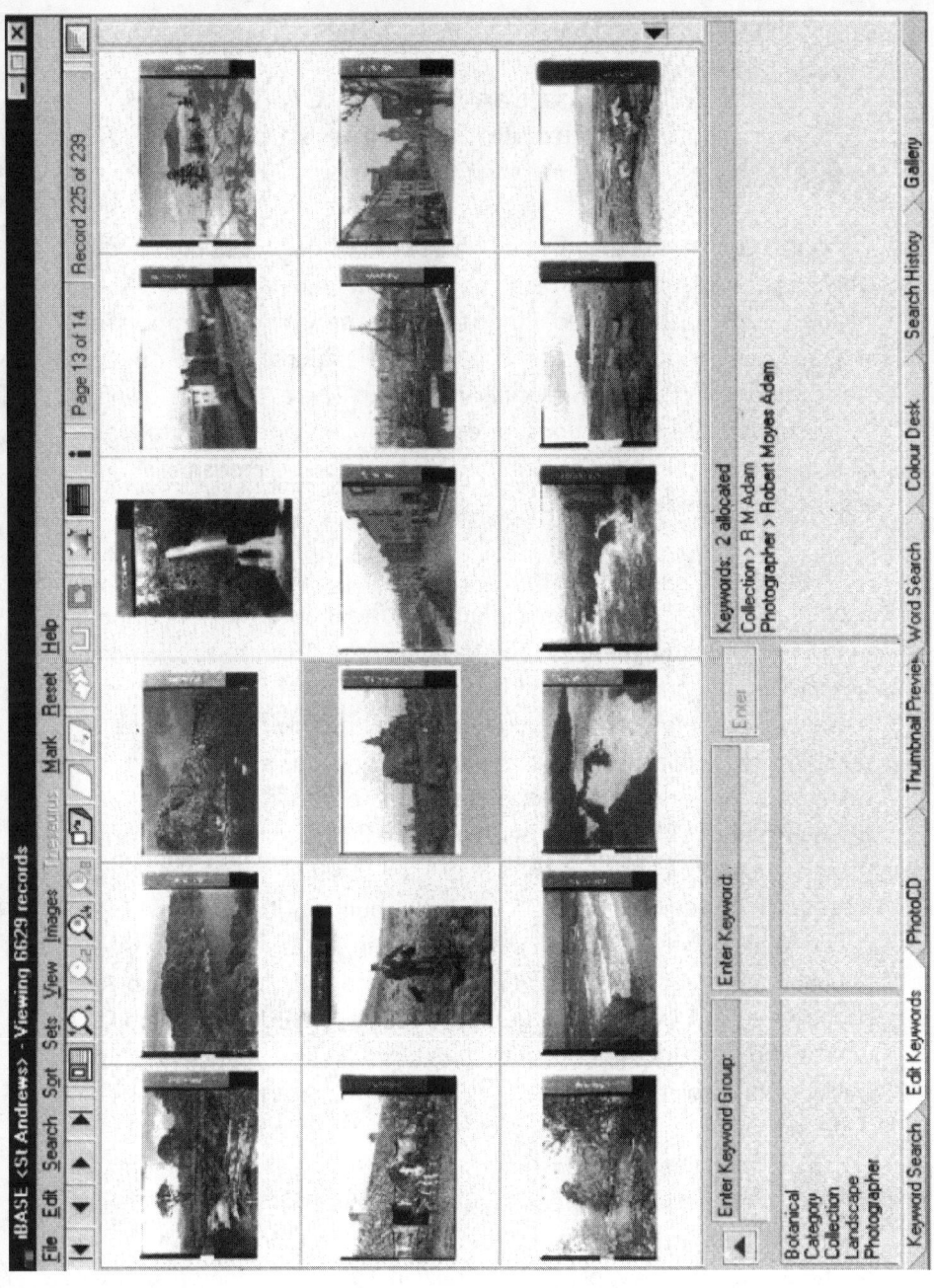

iBase: gallery screen

The National Historic Ships Project

R G W Prescott and Deanna Groom,
Scottish Institute of Maritime Studies,
University of St Andrews

Introduction

This paper describes a project to create a database of surviving historic ships in the United Kingdom, thus providing an important management tool in the development of national policy on the preservation of historically significant ships. The experience gained in this project has implications for others who are working with large-scale, geographically distributed, transport, industrial and engineering heritage collections.

Throughout the historical period ships and sea-faring have played a central role in the social and industrial history of the United Kingdom (UK) and these islands have witnessed the birth of many new developments in ship and boat-building, naval architecture and maritime technology. It is therefore not surprising that we have in the UK a rich collection of surviving ships and boats from the past, many of which are the subject of attempts to preserve and interpret them as part of our maritime heritage. The first successful attempt to preserve a historic ship in the UK began in 1922 when the Royal Navy decided to preserve HMS VICTORY, built at Chatham in 1765, by bringing her ashore to a graving dock in Portsmouth Dockyard. Today, after extensive and ongoing restoration work, she provides for both the Royal Navy and the general public a reminder of past naval glories and an inspiration for the future. Since then, numerous ship-preservation projects have been set up with the intention of saving a wide range of different types of vessels, including, for example, warships, merchantmen, passenger vessels, fishing vessels, lifeboats, harbour service craft and recreational craft (Brouwer, 1993). These preserved ships and boats are a distinctive and important part of the heritage scene. They play a key role in the interpretation of our maritime past for researchers and those involved in education, leisure and tourism activities.

The proliferation of ship preservation projects has not been without problems. Ships were not built with great longevity in mind (30-50 years would be a good average life span for most vessels) and they are constructed of more ephemeral materials than are many buildings and industrial monuments. They also present special conservation problems when removed and preserved apart from their natural operating environment. These factors contribute to the great cost of ship preservation projects, which, for the largest vessels, can run to millions of pounds (Prescott, 1998). Furthermore, the selection of ships for preservation has generally been idiosyncratic and unplanned, with the resultant danger that scarce resources may not be applied in the most efficient manner in the national interest.

Recognizing that these problems could lead to unfettered competition for over-stretched and finite resources, a new independent body, the National Historic Ships Committee (NHSC) was set up in 1992 with the brief to develop national policy guidelines on the preservation of historic ships and boats. The Committee has won broad support for its work, and provides a source of independent advice on historic ship preservation in the UK for central government and heritage funding agencies.

NHSC commissioned the National Historic Ships Project (NHSP) in 1995 to research information on historic ships surviving in the UK, to develop a method of evaluating historical significance in ships and to prepare guidance on best practice in the restoration of historic vessels (Allen and Prescott, 1996).

The National Register of Historic Vessels
The NHSP has at its heart a database of surviving British-built vessels over 40 feet (12.19m) or 40 tons displacement which were built before 1946 and are still lying, substantially intact, in British waters.

This database, the National Register of Historic Vessels (NRHV) contains detailed information about the construction, history and present-day management of more than 1,700 vessels and under-pins the advice given by NHSC on historic ship matters. At present the NRHV functions primarily as a heritage management tool, though the amount and the complexity of the information stored in the database will increasingly lead to its appreciation as a research and information source by a wider range of users. However, as with most museum-based collections, its usefulness as a research instrument must reflect the fact that the resource-base encompasses only those items that have enjoyed the accident of survival to the present day. The NRHV is not to be thought of as a representative sample of all previous British-built ships and boats.

Database Design

The National Register was set up as a relational database using a commercially available software package (currently Microsoft ACCESS). A significant amount of additional programming was required in order to tailor the package to our needs, particularly where the design of suitable data-entry forms and standard queries which could be addressed to the database were concerned. The principal classification system we have used for historic vessels is based on a hierarchically arranged functional thesaurus which covers the full range of functions that ships and boats have been required to perform. The use of this functional classification system has been of great value in developing concepts such as the *UK Core Collection of Historic Vessels* (see below). We have used a simplified version of the maritime section of the thesaurus of monument types developed for the Royal Commission on the Historical Monuments of England (RCHME, 1995). The section of the thesaurus covering Fishing Vessels is set out below as an example:

```
MARITIME CRAFT
   FISHING VESSEL
      FISHING DREDGER
         OYSTER DREDGER
      LINE FISHING BOAT
         LONG LINER
      NET FISHING BOAT
         DRIFTER
         SEINER
         TRAWLER
         POT HAULER
      SEAL FISHERIES VESSEL
      WHALER
         WHALE CATCHER ...
```

Because of the hierarchical nature of the classification, vessels may be entered, and searches made, at any level within the system depending upon the information that is to hand. This is an advantage in cases where insufficient information is known about a vessel. Take the case of a vessel used at the end of her life, in a much-altered state, as a houseboat. Close inspection may reveal that her hull is typologically a fishing vessel, possibly even a net fishing boat, but there may not be sufficient evidence to say whether she was a drifter, trawler or seiner. Such a controlled language thesaurus also avoids the ambiguities associated with the numerous and relatively imprecise "type" labels that are frequently used to describe ships and boats (e.g., *Fifie*, *Smack*, *Nickey* and *Zulu* are all regional names that have been applied to the functional category 'drifter'). Although in a rigorous system of classification it is necessary to eschew these popular vernacular terms they have a research value for ethnologists and we have included them in the database as supplementary information. It is possible to search the database using these terms.

The fields of data recorded for each entry in the database include the following (all this information is not necessarily available for each vessel):

Vessel name(s)
Function(s)
Date and place of build
Builder
Construction materials
Dimensions and tonnage
Propulsion system
Current location
Owner(s) and Manager(s)
Vessel history (a free text field)
Bibliographical sources
Archival deposits related to the vessel
Management fields relating to funding history, NHSC deliberations etc.

Ships and boats are continuously modified throughout their working lives and we therefore record start and end dates for most of the information entered on the database. In this way a formal history of the vessel is built up to complement the narrative history which is stored in the free-text history field. Where possible, we store a digitized image or images of the vessel. This feature is important given the size of the Register, for once one departs from the few large and well-known ships such as the clipper ship CUTTY SARK, Brunel's steamship GREAT BRITAIN and HMS BELFAST most users will not recognize a ship or boat from its name alone, indeed in the case of fishing vessels and yachts there are examples of a number of vessels sharing a common name. Reference to an image is a helpful way of sorting out vessels in such cases.

Because the Register is designed to hold information about owners and managers of historic vessels it has been necessary to register the project under the terms of the Data Protection Act 1984 (revised 1998).

Assembling Data for Entry

Gathering information about historic ships for entry on the Register is a complex process. It includes the extraction of data from various Vessel Registry documents, museum accession registers, vessel lists compiled by specialist clubs and associations (e.g., the Steamboat Association of Great Britain, and the Association of Dunkirk Little Ships) and a variety of shipping publications. In addition, targeted fieldwork at key locations around the coast has been important, particularly in locating privately-owned vessels and vessels that have been abandoned or "hulked". In some cases these apparently lost causes can be rescued and brought back to a useful life by local bands of enthusiasts. Privately owned vessels greatly out-number museum or trust-owned vessels on the Register and present special problems for the project team. Opening communication with their owners (a necessary precursor to obtaining detailed information about these vessels) has posed serious difficulties. Our reaction to these difficulties has been to launch a publicity campaign encouraging private owners to register their boats. This campaign centres upon the issue of a handsome certificate as an incentive to owners to complete our detailed registration form. We also publish a newsletter, SCANTLINGS, which is sent to all owners who submit completed registration documents. The response to this publicity campaign has been good and has resulted in the receipt of many new registrations.

With so many routes whereby data may be obtained it is important to record in the Register the nature of the source for each entry. The project team prefers to verify information by a personal inspection of each vessel but this is possible in only a minority of cases. However, for each entry, the Register indicates the authority for the information it contains.

Using these methods, data on approximately 1,700 vessels have been acquired for entry to the Register. Space does not permit an extensive description of the ships on the Register but suffice to say that the number of vessels recorded exceeds by an order of magnitude the best informed estimates held by NHSC at the start of the project. The vessels range in age from the seventeenth to the twentieth century and include examples powered by sail and oar, steam and motor. The range of building materials used in their construction includes wood, iron, steel and concrete (the latter a new contribution to shipbuilding technology in the twentieth century).

Using the Database: The Derivation of the *UK Core Collection of Historic Vessels*

The relational properties of the database make it possible to answer a wide range of questions about the historic ship resource. Thus, for example, it is possible to obtain a list of those surviving vessels which were engaged in the Dunkirk evacuation which are currently based in Scotland; or one can obtain information about the proportion of any functional category of vessels which is privately-owned (or is steam-powered and built on the Clyde, and so forth). The range of information that can be explored via the database is extensive.

A key objective set by NHSC when initiating the National Historic Ships Project was a plan to identify a group of vessels of pre-eminently national or international significance in terms of their heritage merit. This concept has been named the *Core Collection of Historic Vessels of the United Kingdom*. Vessels on this *Core Collection* *(CC)* should be so significant that every effort should be exerted nationally to ensure their survival in a good state. In developing the CC the project team took as their starting point a quotation from the evidence given by NHSC before the Parliamentary Committee enquiring into the management and care of the nation's heritage:

> *"[The Core Collection] should span and chronicle the spectrum of achievement in our Maritime History as well as the changes in construction and associated technology..."*

We interpreted this statement to mean that we should pay attention to the full range of functions which ships and boats are asked to perform, ensuring that no major function is overlooked. Such a concern for function is a central feature of the NRHV database. Its use emphazises that, in general terms, the smaller vernacular boats of our fishing fleets and our harbour service craft are in their way just as important to our maritime heritage as the larger and perhaps more prestigious ships of the Royal Navy and the ocean-going Merchant Navy. We therefore consulted the NRHV to extract lists of vessels from each functional category. The next step was to select from each of these data sets vessels which seemed to be of pre-eminent heritage merit. For this purpose we developed a method for assessing historical significance which quantifies fourteen separate aspects of the vessel and her preservation project. The elements of this system are listed below:

Vessel Attributes:

1	Technological innovation
2	Exemplary status - type and construction
3	Exemplary status - function
4	Aesthetic impact
5	Historical associations with significant people and events
6	Socio-economic associations
7	Percentage originality of fabric (referred to the end of the vessel's working life)
8	Condition
9	Age
10	Scarcity of vessel type
11	Scarcity of vessel function

Project variables:

12	Preservation strategy
13	Project technology
14	Project management

Vessels are quantitatively evaluated on each of these dimensions, the necessary information being obtained from the detailed records in the database. Considerable exercise of judgment is needed at this stage. Inspection of the records in the database for each ship in a particular functional category quickly thins down the field of potential candidates for the CC. The evaluation formula is then applied to the remaining ships and boats and a short list of candidates for the CC is developed for consideration by NHSC. Where possible, this list should encompass the historical range of technical variation found in each functional category (e.g., the transition from sail to steam and motor power in fishing vessels, or the shift from wood to composite construction, iron and steel and concrete in ship-building). Of course, some decisions about significance are difficult to make. Furthermore, we recognize that some vessels selected for the CC may well be lost to the heritage at some point by accident or other circumstances. We have therefore proposed an additional list of *Designated Vessels (DV)* which, while not being put forward as candidates for the CC, are acknowledged as having substantial heritage merit. Some of these vessels may in future be admitted to the CC.

Using the above procedure NHSC approved draft lists of vessels for the CC and the *DV* lists in November 1999. The draft CC comprises 46 vessels (see Table 1), the draft *DV* list comprises a further 157vessels. The lists are to be regarded as draft lists for a period of six months during which time they will be debated at a series of public meetings. These meetings will provide opportunities for the maritime heritage constituency, museums, vessel owners and funding bodies, to influence the final composition of the *Core Collection* and the *Designated Vessels* list. Once finally agreed, it is expected that the lists will have a considerable influence on the future management of our maritime heritage.

Future Developments
These are likely to address the following three aspects of the NRHV:

a) The quality of information in the NRHV

The reliability of any database is dependent upon regular checking and up-dating of entries. This is particularly important when dealing with ships and boats, which may be bought and sold, moved from place to place, structurally modified for new purposes or destroyed by stress of weather. Recommendations will therefore be made for a rolling programme to review the data on the Register at regular intervals.

b) The criteria for inclusion of vessels in the NRHV:

NHSC is already under pressure to amend the NRHV criteria so as to include smaller and younger vessels. At present the size criterion used in the NRHV discriminates against large numbers of significant but small vernacular craft. Similarly, the age criterion excludes a number of significant new designs that have appeared since 1945, e.g., the Arun class lifeboats of the Royal National Lifeboat Institution. Relaxing the present criteria will substantially increase the number of vessels eligible for inclusion on the NRHV, thereby increasing its potential as a research instrument.

c) The question of public access to the NRHV database.

At present the database is maintained on a stand-alone PC, though the CC and DV lists have been posted on the NHSC web-site. In the next phase of the project steps will be taken to make the NRHV accessible to a wider range of users. Initially, edited sections of the database will be published on the Internet. For example, lists of museum-ships open to the public, or lists of historic vessels which are available for charter, could be promulgated. These would be offered as flat files. However, eventually it is hoped to move to a position in which fuller access to the database can be provided. Some sections of the database will always have to remain restricted because they hold privileged, confidential information about individuals or financial matters. However, these exceptions apart, it remains our goal to move towards a position in which users can engage in dynamic queries which utilise the full potential of the database, via the Internet. Such a move will herald a shift in emphasis for the NRHV, away from a cultural resource management tool towards becoming a more versatile research instrument.

Acknowledgments

We thank Dr Julian Crowe, the Officers and members of the National Historic Ships Committee and the owners and managers of the vessels on the database for their assistance with this project, which was supported by grants from the Department of Culture Media and Sport, the Heritage Lottery Fund and the National Maritime Museum.

References

Allen, C. G. and Prescott, R.G.W. (1996), Towards a national policy on historic ships: research projects sponsored by the National Historic Ships Committee; paper in *Historic Ships: Design, Restoration and Maintenance,* Royal Institution of Naval Architects, London.

Brouwer, N. J. (1993), *International Register of Historic Ships,* Oswestry.

Prescott, R. G. W. (1998), The role of ships within dockyard redevelopment: enhancement or embarrassment? Paper in *Rendoc '98: Proceedings of the First Conference on Dockyard Redevelopment,* CHDT, Chatham

RCHME (1995), *Thesaurus of Monument Types: a Standard for Use in Archaeological and Architectural Records,* RCHME & English Heritage, London.

Table 1: The proposed list of the *Core Collection of the Historic Vessels of the United Kingdom*:

Functional category (No. on NRHV)	*Vessel*	*Location*	*Description*
Channel clearance (30)	**BERTHA** Built: c1844 Bristol	Bristol	The Bridgewater drag boat, probably to Brunel's design. May be the oldest steam powered vessel in the world
Coastguard craft (1)	**VIGILANT** Built: 1902 Falmouth	Portsmouth	Auxiliary sail and steam revenue cutter, the last to carry sail. Fine Edwardian decor. Sole survivor of the 1919 Spithead Review
Communication craft	None at present	-	-
Experimental craft (6)	**TURBINIA** Built: 1893-4 Wallsend upon Tyne	Newcastle	Charles Parsons' experimental test bed for marine turbine power. Appeared (at great speed) at Queen Victoria's Diamond Jubilee Naval Review, Spithead in 1897
Factory ships	None at present	-	-
Fighting ships (160)	**ALLIANCE** Built: 1945 Barrow	Gosport,	A-class fleet submarine from the Second World War, designed for service in the Pacific
	BELFAST Built: 1938 Belfast	London	6" gun cruiser. Her Second World War service included Arctic convoy duties and service in the Far East

Functional category	Vessel	Location	Description
	HMS CAROLINE Built: 1914 Birkenhead	Belfast	A light cruiser, the sole surviving veteran of the Battle of Jutland. Still in commission with the Royal Navy as a drill ship for the RNR
	CMB4 Built:1916 Hampton	Duxford,	30 knot shallow draught motor boat carrying a single torpedo.
	GANNET Built: 1878 Sheerness	Chatham	"Dotterel" class steam and sail sloop, barque rigged and capable of 11.5 knots under steam power. Carried out policing duties throughout the Empire
	HSL 102 Built: 1936 Hythe	Cruising, based on the Solent	Fast air-sea rescue launch for the RAF. Took part in the Dunkirk evacuation in 1940
	HOLLAND I Built: 1901 Barrow	Gosport	The Royal Navy's first submarine, built under licence to the design of the Irish-American J P Holland
	LANDFALL (LCT 7074 Built: 1944 Hepburn	Birkenhead	Tank landing craft, one of the largest of the amphibious warfare vessels built for the Royal Navy during World War II and fore-runner of the modern ro-ro ferry

Functional category	*Vessel*	*Location*	*Description*
	MINERVA (M33) Built: 1915 Belfast	Portsmouth	A shallow draught monitor armed with 6" guns for coastal bombardment. She saw service at Gallipoli and in the White Sea
	MTB 102 Built: 1937 Portsmouth	Ipswich	Prototype of the Vosper-built MTB's, capable of 40 knot speeds. A veteran of Dunkirk
	T3 Built: c 1917 Richborough	Yeovilton	One of a fleet of 45 seaplane lighters developed for the Royal Navy. Towed at speed by warships, they carried a Sopwith Camel which could take off while the lighter was under way. They were the first aircraft carriers in the Royal Navy
	UNICORN Built: 1824 Chatham	Dundee	A "*Leda*" class frigate built to the Seppings system of construction. She required very little repair in her long life "*in ordinary*" and as a drill ship, with the result that she is in a remarkably original state.
	HMS VICTORY Built 1765 Chathams	Portsmouth	A first-rate ship of the line, Nelson's flagship at the Battle of Trafalgar. She is still in commission as the flagship of the Commander-in-Chief.

Functional category	Vessel	Location	Description
	WARRIOR Built: 1860 Blackwall	Portsmouth ·	The Royal Navy's first "*ironclad*" and a vessel whose design transformed naval warfare
Fishery protection craft	None at present	-	-
Fishing vessels (322)	**EXCELSIOR** Lowestoft Built: 1921	Cruising, based Lowestoft	A sailing trawler of the type once common throughout the UK fishing fleet
	EXCELLENT Built: 1931 Sandhaven	(Private ownership, still fishing)	A motor fishing vessel with a long record of continuous service
	LIVELY HOPE Built: 1936 Cockenzie	Anstruther,	A ring-net fishing vessel
	LYDIA EVA Built: 1930 Kings Lynn ·	Gt Yarmouth	A steam drifter of a type once numerous in the North Sea herring fishery
	REAPER Built: 1902 Sandhaven	Anstruther,	A sailing herring drifter of the Scottish "*fifie*" type
	STORMY PETREL Built: 1890 Whitstable	(private ownership)	A Whitstable oyster dredger, built to work the famous North Kent oyster beds
Houseboat (86)	None at present	-	-

Functional category	Vessel	Location	Description
Leisure craft (287)	**BRANKSOME** Built: 1896 Windermere	Windermere	An elegant Victorian lake steamer in largely original condition.
	CORRIE Built: 1908 Sandbanks	(private ownership)	An Edwardian racing yacht
Mission vessel	None at present	-	-
Research vessel (8)	**DISCOVERY** Built: 1901 Dundee	Dundee	A purpose-designed research vessel, built to the general configuration of a barque-rigged auxiliary steam whaler. Saw wide service in polar region exploration
Safety craft (133)	**ALFRED CORRY** Built: 1893 Gt Yarmouth	Southwold	A sailing lifeboat built by Beeching of Great Yarmouth for off-shore rescue work
	JESSE LUMB Built: 1939 Cowes	Duxford	A Watson twin screw motor lifeboat
Service craft (260)	**CALSHOT** Built: 1931 Southampton	Southampton	A tug-tender of the type that served great ocean liners, including the QUEEN MARY and QUEEN ELIZABETH
	JOHN H AMOS Built: 1931 Paisley	(private ownership)	A paddle tug for the River Tees Commissioners, she is the sole remaining paddle tug on the NRHV

Functional category	Vessel	Location	Description
	LV91 (Helwick) Built: 1937 Dartmouth	Swansea	A Trinity House light-vessel
	MAYFLOWER Built: 1861 Bristol	Bristol	A steam-powered river tug which worked commercially for over 100 years.
	OLGA Built: 1910 Porthleven	Swansea	A sailing pilot cutter, working originally out of Barry
	PYRONAUT Built: 1934 Bristol	Bristol	A diesel-powered fire float, specially designed to be able to work under the bridges crossing the Floating Harbour at Bristol
	SABRINA Built: 1870 Gloucester	(private ownership)	A steam-powered inspection craft of riveted iron construction, built for the Directors of the Gloucester & Berkeley Canal Company
Training ship (32)	None at present	-	-
Transport craft – cargo (251)	CABBY Built: 1928 Rochester	(private ownership)	A spritsail barge working between London and the Kent and Essex ports. She has remained in the ownership of commercial shipping companies throughout her life

Functional category	Vessel	Location	Description
	COMRADE Built: 1923	Cruising, River Humber	A square-rigged Humber sailing keel.
	CUTTY SARK Built: 1869 Dumbarton	Greenwich	A composite-construction sailing clipper built for the China tea trade
Transport craft – cargo (contd.) (251)	**GLENLEE** Built: 1896 Port Glasgow	Glasgow	A Clyde-built steel sailing barque, representative of the last generation of sailing cargo carriers
	PEACOCK Built: 1915 Birmingham	Birmingham	A canal narrowboat built for Fellowes, Morton & Clayton. She has iron sides and an elm bottom, a traditional build for her type
	RESULT Built: 1893 Carrickfergus	Belfast	A steel, three-masted topsail schooner built to carry cargo in the coasting trade
	ROBIN Built: 1890 Blackwall	London	A steel steamer, representative of vessels employed in the tramping cargo trades
Transport craft – ceremonial (7)	**PRINCE FREDERICK'S BARGE** Built: 1732 London	Greenwich	A highly ornate Royal row-barge for the Prince of Wales, with carved and guilded decoration designed by William Kent and executed by James Richards et al

Functional category	Vessel	Location	Description
Transport craft – passenger (194)	**CITY OF ADELAIDE** Built: 1864 Sunderland	Irvine	A composite construction emigrant sailing ship which plied between the UK and Australia. She also served as an RNVR drill ship on the Clyde
	GREAT BRITAIN Built: 1843 Bristol	Bristol	Brunel's great trans-Atlantic liner, the first ocean-going, iron, screw steamship to be built. She also has a multi-masted schooner rig
	KINGSWEAR CASTLE Built: 1924 Dartmouth	Cruising, based Chatham	A paddle steamer built for passenger carrying on the River Dart
Waste disposal vessel (1)	None at present		

Digitizing the Scottish Wills

George MacKenzie
National Archives of Scotland
Edinburgh

Introduction

The project to create digital images of all the wills recorded in Scotland up to 1875 is part of a larger initiative, the Scottish Archive Network. With the aim of opening up access to Scotland's rich archival heritage using the Internet, this is a three-year, £4 million project involving virtually every archive in Scotland and employing fourteen full-time staff. The Heritage Lottery Fund is providing 75 per cent of the costs, with the balance coming roughly equally from the National Archives of Scotland(NAS) and the Genealogical Society of Utah (GSU). The wills are one of the three parts of the Scottish Archive Network – the others being catalogues, and special archive services. The relationship between these reflects the way in which the project concept developed.

A Union Catalogue of Scottish Archives

Starting from the premise that potential users do not really know what is in Scottish archives, or where it is located, and that even when they do, existing paper catalogues may be difficult to search, owing to their complexity or size, the project will create top level descriptions of every fonds (or collection of archival documents) held in the forty seven participating archives, and make this union catalogue available for electronic searching.

A number of similar cataloguing initiatives is underway in the United Kingdom, stimulated by the technological opportunities offered by the Internet. The Scottish Archive Network is more advanced than others and has some unique advantages. First, it is a single project and has its funding already in place, ensuring that it can achieve its stated objectives. Second, the scale of archives in

Scotland is manageable. The top level catalogues of the participating archives can all be accommodated on a single server, thus avoiding problems of complex searching protocols. Third, a dedicated team of four project staff will create the catalogue descriptions, thus ensuring a far higher degree of consistency than would be possible if all forty seven participating archives created their own. Fourth, by providing additional services, the Scottish Archive Network will be more attractive to users.

The top level descriptions will include:

- the name of the collection or funds,
- the covering dates,
- a brief administrative history of the organisation or a biography of the family or individual who created it, and
- a summary of the contents

following internationally agreed archival standards (The International Standard of Archival Description (General) or ISAD(G) and the International Standard for Archival Authority Records (Corporate, Personal and Family) or ISAAR(CPF) produced by the International Council on Archives. Copies are available on its website) The top level descriptions will provide a gateway to more detailed information, where it exists. In some cases there will be a hyperlink to the electronic catalogue of a participating archive, while in others the user will be advised to contact the archive by e-mail for more information.

A Virtual Reference Desk

The second main part of the Scottish Archive Network is a series of special archive services. The concept behind these is that searching on the Internet is not like visiting an archive. For one thing it is far easier to do, and will attract far more people, many of whom have no experience and no knowledge of what an archive is. For another, there is no archivist available at the reference desk, filtering inquiries, and pointing researchers in the right direction. To fill this gap we need a virtual reference desk with simple, intuitive functions.

The core of this service we call the Knowledge Base. Borrowing the techniques of Knowledge Management, this will gather material from existing files, notebooks and reference documents in archives and from the experience of individual archivists, to produce an electronic encyclopaedia on Scottish archives and Scottish history. Entries will be split into a topic page with general information and a key image on the topic, and a frequently-asked questions (FAQ) page with further sources for study, both primary and secondary. The Knowledge Base will be dynamic, so that every time a member of staff of a participating archive answers a new question of substance, that answer can be submitted for addition to the Knowledge Base.

Linked to the Knowledge Base will be other services, including an electronic discussion group, which will act like a virtual coffee machine, around which archive staff and readers gather to swap sources, ask questions and float ideas. A Yellow Pages reference section, of information about Scottish archives, including opening times, locations and services available, will complement the Knowledge Base. There will be virtual exhibitions, partly based on exhibitions already mounted in Scottish archives, edited to take account of the different format and audience of the Internet. A bookshop will feature the publications of participating archives. With the recent leaps in e-commerce, this may change from the shop window that was originally conceived, to a virtual shop which does sell publications.

The Wills – a Major National Resource
The third part of the Scottish Archive Network is the wills. The concept was to add a resource which would be of maximum value to potential users. Since around half of today's users of archive services in Scotland are interested in genealogy, the answer was a

comprehensive index to the wills. Despite the popularity of this group of records, and their national significance, for they cover the whole of the country, no comprehensive index exists before 1876. As they are public records, there were no copyright issues to be resolved.

However, to provide an improved index to an already very popular range of records would have placed intolerable strain both on the staff of the NAS and on the records themselves, which show signs of wear from overuse in the past few decades. Therefore, the idea developed of creating digital images, to reduce repetitive demands on staff time, and to ease the pressure on the original documents.

The wills, or testaments to give them their proper name, are a unique resource for historical study. Scots law distinguishes between heritable and moveable rights, the former covering land and buildings, the latter covering goods, money and other possessions. Testaments are exclusively concerned with moveable rights and consist of three elements. First is the confirmation of the identity of the executor of the deceased's moveable estate. If the deceased has nominated an executor, this is known as a *testament testamentar*; if the deceased died intestate, the executor is appointed by the court and this is known as a *testament dative*. Second is an inventory of the estate. Third is a will, if the deceased left one.

Until the 1820s responsibility for administering succession to moveable property   rested with the commissary court, a legacy from the pre-Reformation church. The commissary courts were based on the dioceses of the medieval period, which bear scant relation to modern county boundaries.   From 1824 jurisdiction shifted to the sheriff courts, though for a considerable period there was an overlap between the old and the new structure. Further details on the new testaments can be found in C.Sinclair.*Tracing Your Scottish Ancestors* (HMSO,1997)

All three elements of the testament can be of historical and genealogical interest. Normally the executor will be a relation of the deceased, and his identity will tell us something about family relationships. In some cases, where the deceased left debts, a creditor could apply to be appointed the executor. If the deceased left a will, then there is considerable genealogical interest in what this contains. But perhaps the richest potential lies in the inventories, which in some cases contain full details of the effects of the deceased, with monetary equivalents. They can give us a snapshot of the contents of a house, or the stock of a merchant, or the tools of a craftsman, with their values. A wide range of occupations is represented among the recorded testaments, and these are a key source for information on economic and social conditions. To give just two examples from Perth in 1727, the inventory of William Allan, maltman, details his distilling equipment and household goods, while the inventory of Robert Peacock, chapman traveller, lists his stock of over forty books and unspecified pamphlets. (Commissariot of Perth, Warrants of Testament, Nationl Archives of Scotland, CC20/6/10).

Testaments are not simply the preserve of the wealthy; some are recorded for people of very modest means. It is clear that testaments exist only for a minority, and that in the majority of cases families simply arranged succession themselves, without the bother and expense of the law. The total number of recorded testaments is not known, but we have estimated that there are 175,000 index entries before 1800 and 300,000 from 1801 to 1876.

Using the Testaments Now

While the testaments are a rich historical source, they are not particularly accessible. For the period up to 1800 there is an alphabetical name index, covering each of the commissary courts (edited by Sir Francis Grant and published by the Scottish Record Society). They contain the name, designation (which sometimes includes occupation) and date of confirmation of the testament. From 1800 to 1823 there are a range of typescript indexes for the different courts. The indexes give the date of confirmation of the testament, and with that information a search can be made in the register of testaments, which are normally, though not invariably, arranged chronologically. From 1824 onward, the recording and indexing format depends on local practice in the sheriff courts. In the larger courts, there are separate series of registers, for confirmations, inventories and wills. Indexing is within the volumes and is of variable quality.

The current system is deficient in a number of ways:
- it only permits name searches;
- several different index volumes may need to be consulted;
- it is complex for readers to understand and takes valuable staff time to explain;
- ordering a volume may take up to 48 hours;
- once the volume is produced, it may still take considerable time to locate the individual testament, as there are no page numbers in the indexes;
- ordering a copy will take around a week;
- ordering a copy by post or e-mail will take two to three weeks.

Moreover, every step in the process involves handling fragile originals.

Stage One : Creating the Index

The first stage is the creation of a single index covering the whole country to 1875. The existing indexes will be keyed by an outside contractor, using photocopies of the index sheets. We require an accuracy of at least 99.99 per cent, which will undoubtedly involve double keying. The many manuscript additions and corrections made to the NAS copies of the index volumes will be added at this stage. Then the index data from the different commissary areas and periods will be combined. This will give a single index that can be searched by name (including patronymic where necessary), date, occupation, place of residence or court of confirmation. It will be a simple matter to search for all bakers in Falkland between 1650 and 1850, or all residents of Stirling.

Stage Two : Image Capture

The second stage is the creation of colour digital images of each page of each register of testaments. The images will be captured in broadly chronological sequence. We estimate there are 350,000 images at the equivalent of A4 size or smaller up to 1800, and 3 million images at the equivalent of A3 size or smaller from 1801 to 1875. Image quality varies considerably within a restricted colour range. Tendering for nine digital cameras is under way, and we have not yet taken a decision on a particular model or models. Our criteria, expressed in the tender document, include speed of image capture across a range of different resolutions and bit depths, the ability to automate a series of camera settings for different types of original, and ease of interface with hardware and software configurations. The target throughput is an average of one image per minute for each of the scanners. We believe this can be achieved, even with relatively high resolutions. Many tasks, such as transferring images to disk, will take place automatically and in the background, thus not interfering with the speed of capture.

The operators will aim for the best image quality possible, but there will be no enhancement of images at the capture stage. Quality control procedures will be developed with the operators, who will be GSU volunteers. They are required always to put preservation of the originals first, followed by image quality and only when those are satisfied is speed of capture to be considered.

Stage Three : Linking the Index to the Image

In the third stage the images will be linked together with the index entries. To do this, the index entries will be reconstituted into court and chronological order, and then presented on screen alongside the captured images. This will give curatorial staff a further opportunity for verifying quality and also for checking the accuracy of the index entries before making the link. If there is no index for an entry, one will be created. We expect to 'retrieve' a number of people who may have been missed or misplaced in the index volumes and therefore lost to history.

Storing and Using the Images

Three image formats will be created: a loss free compressed TIFF (tagged image format file) image for long term storage purposes (TIFF v.6.0 with LZW compression), a JPEG (Joint Photographic Experts' Group) compressed file for consultation, and a JPEG grayscale file for use by the GSU. Holding the images in more than one format gives additional choices for future migration to new formats. As a security measure, the contract between the GSU and Scottish Archive Network Ltd gives either party the right to derive an image from the other's holdings at cost price.

A range of data will be automatically generated about the images. This metadata will be both administrative and technical, and will be kept in separate databases, using the image file number as the link. The file number will follow the existing document reference. The data will include the document reference number, the date of image capture, the resolution, the camera and light settings. This will be invisible to the user, but available in the event of any future queries or problems of quality control relating to the capture process.

The TIFF images, which will average 10 megabytes, will be held off line on DLT (digital linear tape). Current products offer up to 35 gigabytes per tape cartridge, which will hold over 3,000 TIFF images. This offers the reassuring prospect of having a physical tape cartridge for each physical record volume. They will be stored in a controlled environment, probably at 15 to 20 degrees Centigrade and a relative humidity of 30 per cent. The JPEG colour images, which will average 300 kilobytes, will be held in mass storage arrays on-line or near-line, with the aim of a maximum access time of 1

146

minute for the user. As technology advances, this is likely to fall significantly. Owing to their size, the images will be available on-line only in the search rooms of the National Archives of Scotland; other users will be able to order copies by e-mail. This too may change with advances in technology.

Preserving the Originals

Preserving the originals is one of the aims of the project and conservation has been given a high priority from the beginning. Three of the 14 full-time staff will be conservators, possibly one of the highest ratios in any archive scanning project. All documents will be withdrawn from public access well before being scanned, to allow strengthening or repair to be carried out as required. Volumes will be broken down only where the binding is not contemporary and where its condition is poor. In all other cases a combination of sophisticated book handling equipment and software will be used to capture the best possible image. Where a volume is broken before scanning, it will be rebound afterwards. All staff and volunteers involved in handling the originals will receive special training, as this is an area where damage can easily occur. Once scanned the originals will be placed in specially-manufactured phase -boxes and will not be available for consultation. An Access database has been set up to provide an audit trail of document movements, from withdrawal from public access, through initial conservation work, to scanning, to permanent storage. This will provide important statistics of workflow and of conservation effort. The preservation aspects of the project will be the subject of a special report.

Using the Testaments In Future

Images of the testaments will be made available to the public towards the end of the project, probably late 2001 or early 2002. The user will be able to search the index in seconds, using any combination of search criteria. Once an entry is located, it will be displayed to a user in the Historical Search Room of the NAS in less than one minute. For a user across the Internet, a copy of the image can be ordered and will be sent by e-mail within a few minutes. At the display and printing stages, a range of simple to use software tools will enable the user to blow up or sharpen the image and to adjust the contrast, brightness and colour balance. This will provide a much better level of access than conventional microfilm copies.

Part of the website will be a help and learning area for the testaments, which will explain the background to their creation, and show the user how to find their way around them. There will be a dictionary of terms encountered in testaments, including a list of occupations, some of which will be unfamiliar to a modern user. There will also be examples of testaments from different periods, and some of famous people, with transcripts.

Rights and Charges

Access to the index and to on-line images in the NAS will be free of charge. Access to the index by Internet will also be free, but copies of images will be charged for, the income helping to fund the future of the network. This exactly duplicates the current charging regime in most archives in Scotland. The project is being run by Scottish Archive Network, a company limited by guarantee with charitable status. The Keeper of the Records of Scotland, who has delegated responsibility from the Queen's Printer for Scotland to administer Crown Copyright in public records, has granted the company a non-exclusive right to create the images and to sell them. The company owns the rights in the image database and the index. The contract between the company and the GSU allows the latter to make the index and grayscale images available for consultation within their family history service, but does not allow them to make copies.

Conclusions

This is probably the largest digital imaging project in archives in the United Kingdom, and is breaking new ground in terms of the organization of workflow, integrating preservation procedures with document handling and image capture in order to protect the originals while achieving a high throughput. It is automating the process as far as possible, in order to promote efficiency and gather management and technical data. The project is also developing standards for image capture and for the metadata that are required to manage long-term access to the digital materials.

By opening a major national resource to wider and more convenient access, and providing an enhanced searching system, the project is benefiting humanities scholars, teachers and pupils and the general public. By linking the testaments with the other parts of the Scottish Archive Network, it is providing a context for wider and deeper exploration and understanding of Scottish history and culture.

Project Design and the Creation of Digital Records in Scotland

Bob Morris
Dept of Economic and Social History
University of Edinburgh

This paper is not about a project, but it will raise a number of issues of project design, potential and methodology which those concerned with the creation, management and presentation of digital resources may wish to bear in mind.

Scottish Nominal Records

A glance at some nineteenth century Scottish gravestones demonstrates some of the issues involved. These gravestones are part of a category of record found across Europe and beyond but, as those who might compare them with English gravestones might remark, they have a number of features in terms of content which are particular to Scotland. The concerns with occupation and recording family members who died in distant parts are rarely found south of the Border. Secondly this is a fine example of nominal record linkage - in this case carried out by the stone mason and relatives - and as such enables us to reconstruct past lives.

In the eighteenth and nineteenth centuries Scotland produced a wide range of nominal records, that is records which attributed a variety of social and economic characteristics to named individuals. Several distinctive series recorded the interaction of the individual and the state through courts and other agencies. This group includes wills and inventories, the saisins (records of real property transactions), sequestration papers and elements of the criminal courts such as precognitions. In a state without a parliament but with its particular legal traditions, these court-based records retained an importance and quality of detail far longer than in the common law regime to the south. Other series came in the nineteenth century, reflecting the information gathering and administrative actions of the modern state, such as the census, the registration of births, deaths and marriages, valuation rolls for local taxes and entry books. At the same time the nominal listings of civil society such as commercial directories, membership lists and subscription lists grew in number and quality. In the European context, Scotland lacks some of the total and sustained record production of the Nordic countries but has a richer and more sustained series than those which relied on the common law system, such as England and Ireland.

Project design can take place only in the context of specific historical enquiries. For Scotland, there are two dimensions to this. First, Scotland was part of the larger processes of industrialization, urbanization and demographic change, but at the same time there were distinctive Scottish features to these processes. Migration played a larger part than in other European countries apart from Ireland and Norway. Urbanization took place more rapidly than any other country has experienced at such a low level of income. Elite social authority was much greater in the countryside than in many other European countries, especially Ireland and England, so that 'surplus' or underemployed people tended to go towards the towns. Wages were lower and house space more limited than in the nearest comparator, England. (Fraser and Morris 1990; Anderson and Morse 1993; Devine 1984; Rodger 1985).

Machine-readable Data Sets

The systematic analysis of the information available in the nominal records of Scotland requires the design and creation of machine-readable data sets. In general this is done project by project. The re-use of existing data sets by historians (unlike the practice of many social scientists) is rare. In part this is a result of the culture of historical research and in part a result of the lack of a significant density of accessible and well-structured public data sets. The initiatives involved in this symposium must pay attention to both these features.

Current historical best practice approaches the preparation of machine-readable data sets from historical records in two basic ways. The first involves records which are systematically structured enabling the historian or archivist to produce a source-orientated data set, in other words, the machine-readable data set mimics the structure of the original record. In some records, such as the parliamentary poll book, a membership list or the valuation roll entry, the data structure is very simple.

400	10	ABBEY	EDWARD	DARLEY ST	BUTCHER	0	1	0
400	10	ABBOT	JOHN	PARK LANE	INNKEEPER	0	1	0
400	10	ABRAHAM	PHINEAS	BRIGGATE	SILVERSMITH & JEWELLER	1	0	0
400	10	ACKROYD	JAMES	WOODHOUSE	STONE MERCHANT	1	0	0
400	10	ACWORTH	JAMES	BLENHEIM SQ	BAPTIST MINISTER	0	1	0

Here the historian has added a code (400) to identify the document, a poll book from an 1834 parliamentary election, and another to identify sections of the document – in this case, the township from which the vote came. In many records the lines and columns of an entry book seem to be waiting for the cells of the spreadsheet to be invented.

Other record structures, like the household entries of the census schedule, are more complex. The hierarchical structure of the relationships involved requires machine-readable structures more complex than the spreadsheet. Information on individuals needs to be linked to household, enumeration district, parish and beyond. The following extract from the 1881 census manuscript of Scotland shows the several levels of information involved.

Dwelling: Renton Barns Farm Cottage
Census Place: Coldingham, Berwick, Scotland
Source: FHL Film 0224030 GRO Ref Volume 732-2 Enum
Dist 1   Page 19

	Marr	Age	Sex	Birthplace
Archibald SHIEL	M	57	M	Dunse, Berwick, Scotland
Rel: Head				
Occ: Shepherd				
Mary A. SHIEL	M	46	F	Penbride, Forfar, Scotland
Rel: Wife				
John SHIEL		12	M	Edrom, Berwick, Scotland
Rel: Son				
Occ: Scholar				
George SHIEL		7	M	Ayton, Berwick, Scotland
Rel: Son				
Occ: Scholar				

The basic structure of the data was given by the document. The problems of analysis included the organization of the data in appropriate fields, the identification of data structures and the creation of metadata for interpretation, notably in coding the information on occupation and place names.

A second group of records provides only unstructured or semi-structured information. The text of a will or that of a precognition of a witness before the Scottish courts are good examples of this. There is no doubt that at some point in the future text analysis will require a machine-readable version of the full text and that key word searches would find machin-readable full text invaluable, but for the purposes of analysis of nominal records of this type the historian must impose structures. One way to do this is to regard the text as the respondent to a questionnaire. If this metaphor is accepted it must be remembered that the historian is not like the social scientist who devises questions to create information. The historian has all the answers and the purpose of the questions is to structure that information.

Nominal Record Linkage

Some records are so rich in content that major gains can be made from analysis of the internal logic of those data, but the most important advances come from nominal record linkage, - the linking of information in two or more records through personal names. Nominal record linkage has been central to historians' use of computers since the 1970s. The basic principles were outlined by Winchester (1970). If entries in a document were associated with individuals with the same or similar names, then there was a strong case for claiming that the information in these entries referred to the same individual. This claim was especially strong when lists were close together in terms of time and space. Rules for linking vary but all seek to avoid two types of error: i) making false links, usually through the existence of multiple common names; and ii) failing to make true links, through name variations. The choice of linkage rules should be influenced by the types of risk which are acceptable to the researcher. (Baskerville *et al.* 1992; Morris 1985; Richardson 1994). The genealogist will want to avoid type one errors and hence seeks the maximum amount of information before making a link. The historian seeking to construct a representative population should be concerned that over elaborate linking rules will introduce systematic bias into the linked population, say towards members of the population who are stable in occupation and dwelling place.

Linked populations form the basis of longitudinal or life history analysis of a wide variety of social and economic experiences in the past. Swedish population registers are some of the most detailed in Europe. Here linkage has been made between entries in the registers to construct the life histories of individuals. Work by Miller (1989) has involved the linking of entries in the registers across the lifetime of each individual involved. These life histories showed not only the importance of frequent migrations within the area studied but also the importance of return migration of individuals who had left the area for a period of residence in (usually) major urban centres. The importance of such frequent movements is difficult to trace as part of a simple comparison of ten-year census schedules.

It is important to recognize some of the many gains in historical knowledge and understanding which have been made through nominal record linkage and the analysis of machine-readable versions of historical records.

Phillips has linked voting records to study the growing importance of party identity within the English electorate (Phillips and Wetherell, 1994). Here simple event history analysis showed that party became more important after the passing of the 1832 Reform Act. Phillips examined the borough constituency of Shrewsbury, which preserved a full run of voting records before and after the Reform Act of 1832. He showed that before 1832 there was a 40% chance of an individual who had once voted tory changing party allegiance. The whigs were more fickle with an 82% chance of change. After the election these hazard rates were reduced to 18% for the tories and 21% for the whigs.

Nenadic (1990, 1992, 1993) demonstrated that the linkage of a number of key Scottish records from the later nineteenth century has made possible important insights in the history of small family firms. Post Office Directories, census manuscript records and the valuation rolls were the major elements of a data set created through letter cluster sampling. This data set demonstrated the short life of

155

most of the businesses involved, the failure of the vast majority to survive the death of the founder and the importance of family capital, labour and networks in the conduct of such business.

In a study of East Lothian farm servants Anthony (1997:207) used the valuation rolls which, by the early twentieth century, tended to name all household heads. Letter cluster sampling (see below) and nominal record linkage enabled him to show, not only the high rate of mobility amongst farm servants, which was already suspected, but also the much lower rates amongst two key groups, shepherds and grieves.

Morton (1999) used poll books, commercial directories, membership and subscription lists to identify the 'active middle class' of Edinburgh in the mid nineteenth century. He was able to describe the occupational structure of that middle class. Lawyers were important but so too were shopkeepers and craftsmen. He showed that lawyers and commercial men did indeed dominate many subscriptions and societies like that for the Relief of Highland Destitution. But there were also associations like that for promoting Schools for Apprentices which were dominated by the craftsmen. This linking of many lists showed overlapping patterns of membership and subscription in which most individuals appeared in one or two lists and a very few had multiple listing. This strategy of nominal linking made possible the identification of activists in the civil society which formed the basis of the recreation of Scottish national identity in the nineteenth century parliament-less nation.

It should be noted here that in recent years computing power has delivered speed and capacity. These features are no longer a major constraint in project design. There exists from the 1970s a (now) faintly comical literature on how to code and abbreviate names and other data.

Inputting Data

The major cost and constraint now lies the inputting of data. Optical character recognition (OCR) techniques are valuable but even when they are appropriate, OCR is still a costly process that requires extensive proof reading. It is an art rather than a science. With many documents, especially those which are hand written or employ older print fonts, OCR is a matter for the future which is likely to employ complex artificial intelligence and pattern recognition techniques. (Coles *et al.* 1997; van Horik 1993) .

Data inputting remains the cost which must make researchers and archivists pause for thought when creating data. The project designer must engage in some form of sampling. Several choices are available.

a) The scientific random sample is of limited value given the need for nominal record linkage. Linking two 10% samples will at best expect to get a 1% linked population even if the two initial populations were identical. Such sampling has the advantage of relating to a wide variety of statistical techniques and could be adequate in situations which required analysis only within one document or looked to linkage with a document available in 100% machine readable form.

b) Since the 1970s historians have tended to use 100% area samples and link records that were close in time and place. This is fine but creates a bias towards the geographically stable and directs the historian towards the spatially-located community as the focus of social action.

c) Since the 1980s attempts have been made to combat some of these drawbacks by letter cluster sampling. This was the strategy used by both Phillips and Nenadic. In essence, letter cluster sampling is a very simple strategy which involves the identification of a population of record entries for sampling by means of the first two or three letters of the surname or patronymic. In some cases sampling might be based on two or more letter clusters. Perhaps the most extensive use of letter cluster sampling was made by Dupaquier and Denis (1992) in a sample of the French population in the nineteenth century. This was based upon 45,000 marriage records which involved a partner with a patronymic beginning with "tra". This strategy increases the efficiency with which many complex records can be searched. It enables individual life histories to be reconstructed in a way which crosses geographical boundaries. The results of this can be important. There are indications that the "tra" sample shows much higher levels of occupational mobility than community studies. This should not be surprising if geographical and occupational movement were linked.

This strategy is very helpful but it remains difficult to evaluate the results coming from the analysis of the resulting populations. In terms of probability theory, it is not clear if N equals the number of cases or N equals the number of letter cluster samples. It is difficult to evaluate the risks of random or of systematic bias which are involved in creating a population in this way. If surname was a socially neutral variable, then N might tend to be nearly equal to the number of cases, but we know that this is not so. The French "tra" sample showed a bias towards certain regions and against names of aristocratic origin. The historian of Scotland knows instinctively that surnames have regional, national, ethnic and language identities. In the heterogeneous populations of large towns, letter cluster samples still have some risk of creating random and hard to estimate bias, but in smaller towns and the countryside the difficulties can be even greater. In the Scottish Borders names such as Armstrong, Turnbull and Walker have clear social meanings.

These concerns reinforce the case for creating a number of 100% machine-readable nominal listings of the Scottish population. The currently available listing of the 1881 census population has immediate potential here (CD-ROM 1). The Scottish wills project could well provide another and different type of listing.(McKenzie, this volume), Such listings will enable the researcher and project designer to achieve two aims. They will provide a base for testing the nature of any given letter cluster sample in terms of key variables. They will also provide a means of tracing the 'leavers' from a geographically- based sample. Selecting and managing such 100% samples must be part of the current debate.

The existence of 100% samples such as the 1881 census and the Scottish wills project will not eliminate the need for 'area' samples nor for historians to take the risks of the letter cluster sample. The 100% listings will enable historians better to evaluate and limit such risks.

Data Sets On-line and on CD-Rom

This final section examines some of the data sets which are available 'on line' and through the medium of CD-ROM and provides a critique of the historian's experience with a view to offering guidance on presentation and selection of materials.

One of the most accomplished data sets available on line is the 1801 census of Norway prepared by Oldervoll and colleagues in the Department of History at Bergen University (Web Site 1). It offers a wide variety of approaches to the data - notably a version with both the front end and the data in English. A coded version of the household database offers a wide range of possibilities. The user can choose country, county or parish level analysis and select variables for cross tabulation. For example, the age structure of household heads may be compared for selected occupational groups. It is possible to view a structured version of the original data but only farm by farm. This is an impressive presentation but there are three criticisms.

i) Access to details of the original occupational code was not easy to find.

ii) When the cross tabulation was prepared on line, it

transferred to the local spreadsheet in a clumsy way which required a variety of clever edits. It did not transfer as a tabbed data set which slid easily into Excel.

iii)   It is difficult to scroll and down load the original set except farm by farm and even in this case it is hard to envisage by chosen farm in the context of the parish as a whole.

As a general lesson here, the archivist who quite properly seeks to assist the user by the provision of facilities such as coding and cross tabulation should still enable the historian user to recreate as far as possible the original document and to mimic the experience of scanning that document. All attempts to standardize or consolidate names, place names or occupational titles should be resisted. Although the archivist may provide occupational coding schemes, indications of the location of placenames (say grid references or historical boundary information), and name standardization dictionaries to assist in on-line searching, as part of the on-line service, this should not preclude schemes of coding and location which the historian wishes to devise, and should be clearly distinct from information provided from the document.

Some of the temptation to provide elaborate front ends may well come from the desire to serve the genealogist with a simple name search. Even in this case many genealogists now seek the context of their ancestor and not the simple identity. To this end the 'neighbours' function of the current 1881 census CD-ROM is an excellent example of a feature which makes it possible to move from the results of a simple name search to data which enables the user the reconstruct most features of the document and thus provide vital context.

Creators of data sets may well be suspicious of the copyright-breaking downloading of huge amounts of data, but growing experience with the registration of data users, together with agreements on data use and the recording of data transfers help to overcome this risk. Audit trails of this type should make it possible to control data use without limiting data access.

As a data set of this nature is explored, the evaluation of results and indeed the selection of data for analysis must depend upon knowledge of the 'area' or parish from which data come or might come. The Scottish researcher will soon have available an on-line version of the two *Statistical Accounts of Scotland* from the 1790s and the 1840s. This takes the form of a type of presentation of digital data which is becoming increasingly common, the image scan of a printed page which has been tagged with a limited number of searchable data fields (such as parish, page number). The user has an extensive amount of data but none of it is machine readable. It is a book on screen. The user is invited to read on screen, or in some cases the 'image' can be down loaded and printed out - in effect an electronic xerox. The user will have to transfer the data to a word file or spreadsheet in much the same way as data are transferred from a xerox or document on the desk top. This is an intermediate technology which will increase data availability but does not have the analytical potential of a machine-readable set like the census. More thought needs to be given to the means by which such data might be interrogated.

A third variety of on-line facility is based upon locality. Such facilities have a variety of motivations, from promoting tourism, urban and regional promotion to education and local historians' enthusiasms. A very fine one based upon the census manuscript for the 'colonies' area of housing in Edinburgh has been prepared for a current (1999) exhibition (Rodger 1999). The example from Pittsburg offers a variety of maps and texts from the city's nineteenth century history (Web Site 2). Some of these features are valuable for an urban historian anywhere in the world. Other features, such as archive catalogue listings would be less relevant for non-local users. In the main the items on these sites are image scans and it is difficult to download copies although easy to print out screenfuls and make notes on screen. The site promises developments in this respect. The archives department of the City of Stockholm has produced a CD-ROM based upon the Roteman population registers (CD-ROM 2). This material is accompanied by an explanation of the Roteman system, maps and descriptions of the neighbourhoods of the city involved together with photographs from the archive. Although limited to a local market - the text is in Swedish - this CD-ROM has already sold well over 2000 copies (CD-ROM 2).

Conclusions

Four conclusions can be derived from this short survey of the issues involved in projects that include the analysis of linkage of nominal records.

i) This survey has clearly identified the value of carefully selected 100% samples, both for direct use in linking and for evaluating letter cluster and area samples constructed for specific projects. The 100% samples will also improve the chances of tracing the geographically mobile - an especially important feature of Scottish experience.

ii) The construction of on-line resources should at all times be document orientated. Fancy front ends and search engines of various kinds do have a value, but the inquirer should at all times have the option of being able to see, if not an image of the original document, at least the data structured and contextualized exactly as in the original document.

iii) Although the emphasis has been on personal nominal data, the use of such data must at all times be tempered and guided by area data. The availability of such data is crucial for the selection of area samples. It will also help with the interpretation of research as varied as the academic case study, the local history and the genealogical enquiry.

iv) Finally attention should be given to locally-prepared data sets, which make it possible to bring together in one 'site' a variety of sources, images, text, nominal listings and archive finding aids. Again, historians should always have access to the structure of the original information and a careful distinction should be made between information added by the archivist and that derived from the original source.

References
Web Sites

1.The Census of Norway from the year 1801, Jan Oldervoll, the Department of History, University of Bergen.
http://www.uib.no/hi/1801page.html

2. Historic Pittsburgh, a joint project of the University of Pittsburgh and the Historical Society of Western Pennsylvania.
http://digital.library.pitt.edu/pittsburgh/

3.The Statistical Accounts of Scotland are at present (Nov 1999) only available in a pre release version. Enquiries to EDINA, Edinburgh University Data Library, Main Library Building, George Square. Edinburgh EH 8 9 LJ.
http://edina.ed.ac.uk/index.shtml

CD-ROMs
1. *1881 British Census and National Index* , available from The Church Distribution Centre, 399 Garretts Green Lane, Sheldon, Birmingham B 33 0 UH.

2. *Söder,* available from City Archives of Stockhom, Computer Department, St Eriksgatan 121, S - 113 43 Stockholm.

Books and Articles

Anderson, M. and Morse, D J.(1993), High fertility, high emigration, low nuptiality: adjustment processes in Scotland's demographic experience' 1861-1914, *Population Studies*, 47, 5-25 and 47, 319-43.

Anthony, R. (1997), *Herds and Hinds. Farm Labour in Lowland Scotland, 1900-1939*, East Linton.

Baskerville, S. W. , Hudson, P. and Morris, R. J. (1992) (eds.)., Record Linkage, *History and Computing* special issue, 4.

Coles, T., Alexander, A. and Shaw, G. (1997) Following the script: Optical Character Recognition Technology and the British Town and Trade Directory, *History and Computing*, 9, 1-16

Devine, T.M. (1984) (ed.), *Farm Servants and Labour in Lowland Scotland, 1770-1914*, Edinburgh.

Dupâquier, J. et Kessler, D.(1992)., *La société française au xixe siècle. Tradition, transitions, transformation*, Paris.

Fraser, W. H. and Morris, R. J. (1990) (Eds.), *People and Society in Scotland, vol. II, 1830-1914*, Edinburgh.

Miller, R., (1989), Cross sectional and longitudinal analysis in historical geographical research - some methodological considerations, in *Studier och handlingar rörande. Stockholms Historia*, VI, Stockholm.

Morris, R J (1985), Does nineteenth century nominal record linkage have lessons for the machine readable century? *Journal of the Society of Archivists*, 7, 503-512.

Morton, G. (1999), *Unionist Nationalism, Governing Urban Scotland, 1830-1860*, East Linton.

Nenadic, S. (1990),The life cycle of firms in late nineteenth century Britain, in Jobert, P. and Moss, M. (eds.), *The Birth and Death of Companies*, Carnforth, 181-96.

—-(1993) The small family firm in Victorian Britain, *Business History*, 35, 86-114.

—- and others(1992) Record linkage and the small family firm: Edinburgh 1861-1891, *Bulletin of the John Rylands Library*, 74, 169-96.

Phillips, J. and Wetherell, C. (1994), Parliamentary politics and municipal politics: 1835 and the party system, *Parliamentary History*, 13, 48-85.

Richardson, S. (1994). Letter Cluster Sampling and Nominal Record Linkage, *History and Computing*, 6, 168-76.

Rodger, R. (1985), Employment, poverty and wages in the Scottish cities, 1841-1914, in Gordon, G. (ed.), *Perspectives of the Scottish City*, Aberdeen.

—-. (1999), *Housing for the People. The Colonies in Edinburgh*, Edinburgh.

Van Horik, R., (1993) Recent progress in the automatic reading of printed historical documents, in Doorn, P. K. and van Horik, R,, Scanning and OCR, special issues of *History and Computing*,5, 68-73.

Winchester, I. (1970), The linkage of historical records by man and computer: techniques and problems, *Journal of Interdisciplinary History*, 1, 107-24.

Closing Remarks

John Arbuthnott
Principal and Vice-Chancellor
University of Strathclyde

Having served as Chairman of the JISC (Joint Information Systems Committee) for four year during which the E-Lib initiative emerged as a crucially important catalyst, I am delighted to have had the pleasure of listening to today's excellent presentations.

Mention of JISC reminds me of the debt we owe to three people who were central to the thrust of debates, plans and actions in the field of digitization and data set management - Lynne Brindley (now Pro Vice Chancellor at Leeds University), Derek Law (now Librarian at Strathclyde University) and Michael Anderson (Professor of Economic and Social History at Edinburgh University).

Today's symposium has given us many examples of on-going projects that are pushing forward the digital resources available to scholars. It has also provided a good deal of practical advice on the key issues that affect the management of such resources. There is no way back and the creation of a real 'Information Society' is dependent on the extensive digitization of our information resources. One of the most astonishing features of the 1990s has been the extent to which fairly large sums of money - overall amounting to hundreds of millions of pounds - have been released by various arms of government for the creation of the content on which the information society will be based. Despite the intense interest and activity in digitization. the amount of material that has been digitized is so far very limited. Selection of material will remain a key issue.

It is important to emphasize that investment in digitization has not been restricted to supporting developments in the scientific research community. Although large sums have gone to create such resources as the Human Genome Project or the Visible Human, this symposium has amply demonstrated the importance of the humanities and the social sciences as sources of primary research material. Making this research material available digitally allows us to unlock the nations's riches and make them accessible through the Internet to a far wider audience than had been thought possible. The drive to meet the needs of that audience will come from (a) the new Scottish Parliament, (b) the rapid increase in awareness of Scotland's cultural resources, (c) the rich new vein of knowledge resource being created in Scotland's network of Science Centres. These three influences will provide a powerful drive in the development of 'Digital Scotland'.

From this symposium there are three major challenges facing us in the management of digital resources'

## 1.	Building coherence and comprehensiveness in the digital resource base.

This symposium demonstrated that we have the building block in place to create an extensive digital 'research library' But the expense involved to create a thoroughly coherent and comprehensive digital resource base does raise questions as to how far the scholarly community, relying on sources from the public sector only, can take this challenge. We need to encourage private sector investment to unlock all of our resources and not just the highlights.

## 2.	Management of relationships

Building Trust

We are fortunate in having a long tradition of co-operation in Scotland and perhaps the best acronyms. Projects and groups as varied as SCONE (Scottish Collections Networked on-line), SCURL (Scottish Convention of University and Research Libraries), SCRAN (Scottish Cultural Resources Access Network) and HEIDS (Higher Education Information Technology Directors in Scotland) demonstrate that commitment to working together.

The recent announcement of the ministerial task force to create 'Digital Scotland' gives us an opportunity to work with other partners cross-sectorally and beyond the universities and scholarly and cultural institutions to business and industry and the nation at large.   Indeed, the 'Digital Scotland' initiative depends on

Government forging partnerships with local communities and the private sector to ensure that new technology will help liberate communities - the universities have a part to play in this.

I can assure you that Government is deadly serious about the demand side of this equation. Access is seen as a major factor in enabling the citizens of Scotland to realise their potential. 'Unlocking' has a 'particular meaning in the eyes of different stakeholders.

3.   Management of Perceptions

Being relevant

These new partnerships will require us to show the relevance of scholarly resources to the Community at large.. Universities have not always been very good at explaining themselves and we must be able to demonstrate why making scholarly resources accessible to a wide audience is of importance. In Tom Devine's recent history of modern Scotland (1999 pix) he says ' the academic community might be accused of introspection at a time when Scotland is entering a phase of historic constitutional change when issues such as identity and culture are being reclaimed and contested both in the media and public debate'. I would argue that bringing the Nation's riches to the nation will be only one part, but an important part, of creating a nation at ease with itself. These resources should not be restricted but widely available to all to enable an informed debate about all aspects of our country's history and society.

The Carnegie Trust, the Royal Society of Edinburgh and other independent scholarly bodies will help - in a limited way through funding but more importantly as advocates of the cause.
Terry Coppock deserves our grateful thank for initiating this most timely conference.

Reference

Devine, T.M. (1999) *The Scottish Nation 1700-2000,* London.

Printed for The Stationery Office Limited 12/99 c5